Diving For Pearls

In Search for Deeper Wisdom

By: Frank Walters

Copyright © 2020 by Frank Walters

ISBN: 9798617413863 (Print edition)

Imprint: Independently published

All rights reserved. No part of this book may be reproduced or used in any manner without written permission of the copyright owner except for the use of quotations in a book review.

Caveat

I violate some conventions in these pages for which I ask the reader's indulgence. My use of capitalization will surely seem excessive to most but I do so with purpose to suggest reverence for first-order principles like Love and Truth and Happiness. Further, I'm afraid I tread on modern-day sensitivities with which I am largely sympathetic. This is a work of decades and may well seem dated to younger readers. I am 90 now, with failing vision, so extensive editing is beyond my ability. I hope the value of the insights outweigh style transgressions.

DIVING FOR PEARLS
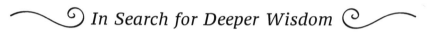
In Search for Deeper Wisdom

Frank Walters

With Book Design by
Josh Cunningham

"If a man is fortunate, he will, before he dies, gather up as much as he can of his civilized heritage and transmit it to his children."

Will Durant
Author of "The Story of Civilization"

DEDICATION

To my children, their children and future generations of offspring:

The parent part of me yearns to live on as a whisper in the consciences of those who follow me to think rightly, live honorably and cherish Truth.

"I read. I study. I examine. I listen. And out of all that I try to form an idea into which I put as much common-sense as possible.

Marquis de Lafayette

INTRODUCTION

Wisdom, like the perfect pearl, is valued because it is both beautiful and rare. Formed and harvested only at challenging depths with great effort and care, it is inaccessible to those insufficiently driven by appreciation of its worth and love for its beauty to bear the burden of its discovery.

We all grow wiser with age. Clearly, then, wisdom is a cumulative process. The trick is to grow wiser faster. The building blocks of wisdom, in essence, are insights. Knowledge helps but without insights it does not lead to wisdom.

So, it is wise to treasure new insights whether consciously or not. The more, the better. The deeper, the richer. They are the building blocks of our wisdom. And cumulative wisdom leads us to better choices and a more self-fulfilling life.

That paragraph in italics above was the first Pearl in what ultimately became an extensive collection of thousands of random and spontaneous insights crafted over the years.

The book you hold in your hand came from collection of thousands of such insights. The one on the back of this book is another.

Each such Pearl began as a full-fledged aphorism or short essay, varying in length from phrase to paragraph to page. The vision then was to capture insights in self-defensive propositions. The goal of each was to unify the logical essentials of some meaningful idea, relying exclusively on reason as the path to Durable Truth.

This book is a compilation of hundreds of such Pearls highly distilled essence of their parent ideas. And since they are boiled down from thoroughly thought-through propositions, they imply far more than their sparse sentences suggest. To the insight-hungry reader that tends to stop you in your tracks and entice you to reflect. That slows reading pace to a crawl. You'll find it is best consumed in small bites.

It might strike you as odd that they are all the same length. This final generation was inspired by the remarkable art of Japanese haiku poetry which is rigidly confined to three lines of five, seven and five syllables. This demands an uncommon compatibility of ruthless rule-based discipline with free, unrestrained creative expression. In haiku that unyielding discipline is a vital part of the art itself.

Here, Pearls in this collection, haiku-like, are condensed to pure essence and restricted to two lines and an averaging 15 words.

This book is dedicated to that task by provoking deeper insights and new angles of thought about a whole host of things.

Every smile, every kindness, every worthy insight shared adds to the sum of Net Good and thereby improves the world. If you find value in this book, please consider recommending it to others, gifting it to those you love and promoting it on social media. With sufficient raindrops, even the arid deserts will bloom.

FRANK WALTERS

We all grow wiser with age for ten ways to grow wiser faster see pages 229-231

WHAT IS AN INSIGHT WORTH?

A single insight can be of incalculable value. It could alter the course of a lifetime. Consider these two Pearls:

Happiness is no random quirk of fate. It is the grand prize of life! Ultimately a choice.

Most never pause to dwell on the transcendent importance of Happiness in the grand scheme of life. But Aristotle thought deeply about it and explained that all things are desired for purpose with a higher purpose ... except Happiness which is desired for its own sake. It is indeed the grand prize of life.

Happiness, then, is the object of all of other desires. That insight—taken to heart—can fundamentally change one's life for the better. That's what an insight can be worth!

Then, there's this related Pearl:

> The two essentials for Happiness are Love and Peace-of-Mind. Love is the easy part.

That insight, if it takes root in your mind, elevates "peace-of-mind" to a first-order objective. It is one of two essentials to Happiness … and the most difficult to achieve. That realization, in turn, provides you a point of attack to greatly enhance your chances for Happiness.

There you have it. In just those two Pearls you have an example of how new insights can enrich your life. Wisdom demands that you optimize your life for Happiness. Seek more insights.

DIVING FOR PEARLS

Wisdom, like the perfect pearl, is beautiful, rare and harvested at challenging depths.

Like a masterpiece in marble, wisdom is crafted one chip of the chisel at a time.

We have it within us to be wiser if we are wise enough to bank & cherish our insights.

Our wisdom lies deep within us as potential yet unmined, like silver still in the mountain.

Pearls are a Lego-like collection of discrete thoughts—building blocks for larger ideas.

Every insight springs to life as another surprise to its author, its source a mystery.

Out of nowhere, a glimpse of Truth pops
into view, like a hummingbird in the mind.

Cherish each insight as a building block of
wisdom. Wisdom is a window to richer life.

Principles, like pearls, should be carefully
chosen, matched, and strung together.

Old is harvest time. Time to gather together
remnants of insights gained and distill Truth.

In the lengthening shadows of twilight,
angled rays of late day sharpen vision.

Every confounding complexity contains
within itself an essence of clear Truth.

The art of wisdom lies in the distillation of
hazy confusion to its core of crystal clarity.

Values are despots; it's true, yet, without
them, Chaos would reign with harsher hand.

Past is past. What, then, of the Future?
Ah, there is Life! All is Potential there!

Each of us sculpts his own destiny using
Choice as his chisel & Will as his hammer.

No one ever became corrupt suddenly.
Going bad? It's a piecemeal deal. Stop.

"Simplify, simplify!" Thoreau exhorts.
Optimize! Optimize! I retort. It is duty.

Brevity is laudable but Clarity is paramount.
Understanding is the goal. Do what it takes.

Principles are synthesized from experience,
constrained by values, magnified by wisdom.

Ignore your wrong self and listen instead to
the noble soul within. Choices are the key.

Willpower is the tiller of life. Without it, we
are adrift on a turbulent sea of raw chance.

To succeed, be taken seriously. Avoid trivial ostentation and pretense. Substance is key.

Wisdom urges us to do what needs to be done when it needs to be done. Get going.

Life is a pyramid. Its base, breadth of choice; its height, longevity. At point, potential ends

---

Teach children to think rightly and they will act nobly on their own. Program for good.

The essential test, always applied before you decide: "At what cost to any freedom?"

Study works of great minds. That practice leads ordinary minds to higher thoughts.

Having brushed against great ideas, we become more than we thought we were.

Clearly, everything has a price. Failure to weigh price almost always carries great cost.

Greed is selfish acquisitiveness. Envy lacks utility and, far worse, it attacks others.

Learn when enough is enough. Restraint strengthens most things. Excess ruins all.

Only the unwise cling to the shallow delights of youth; our potentials surpass our dreams.

Choose to cherish Truth as a first-order principle of life. Truth trumps all virtues.

Honor in all things. Let that be a beacon for your life. You will thereby avoid the rocks.

However afflicted, each of us has the power to be much stronger through our Will alone.

Life is a turbulent sea, roiled and churned by an ebb and flow of eternal Cause and Effect.

It is an observable moral imperative for each living thing to strive to thrive. Do your part.

He who steals the peace in my mind steals my happiness—a felony. Mind Peace is key.

To understand what folks truly believe, examine their actions. What they say won't.

Even among rotten options, there is always a best way. Choose the one most likely that.

Mine each experience for enduring principle. Mistakes are the most instructive of all.

Evil consequence is poorly defended by righteous good intention. Results matter.

Only the willfully blind never question their own favorite visions. It's best to test often.

Each generation is duty-bound to carry forward the cherished lessons of its tribe.

Whatever we have in this life is worth only the value we give it. Cherish the right things.

A dark disposition is a self-inflicted wound; think it gone. How you think is who you are.

Touching any life leaves an indelible mark. Touch gently. Especially those you love.

It is far better to be, then not be, than to never have been. (Good advice for cows.)

Progress by all means ... but carefully; our ancestors were not all fools. Keep the best.

Life is like a fisherman's backlash: Every reel knot grows tighter as it nears its hard core.

There is no choice without cost. Cost is a universal constant. Calculate it carefully.

Attitude, Talent and Luck influence success. Of the three, only Attitude offers a choice.

Truth is truth. Gold is gold. Either way, the value is intrinsic, wherever it can be found.

Every human life is sculptured in tiny increments, one chisel chip at a time.

Between Conflict and Tolerance lies a better choice: Reasoned Persuasion works best.

Facile phrases are would-be tyrants. Shortcuts for thought, slogans deceive.

When rationality surrenders to emotion, danger lurks. Understand, think, then act.

Our values live on as a whisper in the consciences of our progeny. Value values.

The greatest threat to happiness is mindless pursuit of pleasure. Durable vs transient.

Soliloquies are our most important discourses, dictating who we are at core.

Never fault those cherished who share your life—especially when fault is warranted.

Forgetting is the ultimate and only true forgiveness. Getting even never works.

Though it is difficult, value your opponents. Their challenge makes you better than ever.

Life is a multiple-choice test. There is always only one best choice; best choose that one.

Learn to know Truth when you see it. Then embrace it as your own. Truth is a treasure.

Every relationship, however close, is but a series of discrete encounters. Value each.

Those who aspire to live honorably make high principle a habit. Habits are tools, too.

To discover potentials, you must first have faith they exist. Faith precedes all discovery.

Any list of high principles begins with Truth. The rest rest upon it. Truth's the foundation.

Learn the lessons of History. Only a fool ignores experience. Ignorance is dangerous.

Beware of those who deceive with the stealthy, devious art of Selective Truth.

Without principles, everything rests on its own considerations. Adlibbed lives fail.

No Self is exempt from the perpetual inner war between Will and Want. Win with Will.

Like fruit, each judgment is best when allowed to ripen until its time. Weigh first.

In sailing, as in life, exult in each perfect but transient moment. Winds change quickly.

Consensus jells slowly and only under cool temperatures. Patience (not easy) prevails.

Life is much like pealing a peach. The longer you keep at it, the harder it is to hang on!

Be not so readily enslaved by trivial possessions. Live content, thus free.

———

Live well. Only a heartbeat separates us from the oblivion of all that used to be.

———

"That's just the way I am!" means that you choose not to change. With will, you can.

———

Calculate consequences, both good and bad. Only then, act. Net good is ever good.

———

The mind can be a fortress if we train it to be a refuge from things beyond our control.

———

Weigh with care the worth of each object, act, thought or character. Only then choose.

———

A dark disposition is just another form of self-mutilation. Attitude is ours to control.

———

Never let your mood to be held hostage by others or circumstance. It is best to be boss.

By force of will alone, you can cultivate a happy disposition within. It is well worth it.

———oOo———

Efficiency is grossly undervalued. Make it a requirement in every task. Waste is near sin.

———oOo———

Trivia is the mortar that cements any human relationship. Share it with those you love.

———oOo———

Frustration, tension, worry and rage change only blood pressure. Keep cool. It pays big.

———oOo———

The liar is condemned by his own transgression. He can trust no one.

———oOo———

Never leave happiness hostage to circumstance. Secure it within.

———oOo———

When you're frustrated and angry.
Ask, "How's this working for me?"

———oOo———

If It is morally wrong to harm others,
surely it is equally wrong to harm oneself.

When shooting an arrow, first take careful aim. Thought precedes act. 1) Think. 2) Do!

It is prudent for a frog to leap without thought, but not you. Be thought full.

Restraint is the essence of art ... and good behavior ... and sound policy ... and all else.

A parent never knows where or when his influence ends. Caring wisdom is key.

To know thyself, look within. Go deep into the dark ... where the harsh Truth hides.

Always, it takes a ton of ordinary to produce an ounce of excellent. Like panning for Gold.

To create strategies for living, allow liferules to guide tactical choice. Take the long view.

Show me a self-wrecked life and I'll show you impulse with freedom to reign over life.

The only just mindset for jury duty is diligent skepticism. As with all critical judgments.

All repetitive conduct becomes, over time, addictive. Addictions become compulsions.

It is a sacred obligation of talent to perform at its limits. Wasting talent is surely sin.

It's safe to assume any display of Confidence will be interpreted by critics as Arrogance.

An empty threat is a promise broken—just another way to lie. So, best avoid promises.

Beware. In the nonentity you may crave lurks the sure loss of your uncertain Self.

What resides inside another's soul is ours neither to change nor blame. Be gentle.

What is is: accept, ignore or change it. But never let it gnaw on your peace-of-mind.

Quick now, list five principles you live by.
Not easy? Better start seriously thinking.

Without Will, what am I? An empty vessel?
An idle thought? Without Will, I'm nothing!

Life's a garden. Cultivate your memories:
weed the weeds, count the blossoms.

Mere human, I credit myself far more than
I have earned and rebuke myself far less.

Never look to a mind ruled by passion for
logical inferences or rational conclusions.

He who would be free submits to no
one—especially the untiring tyrant: Self.

Flip side: Happiness owes more to Optimism
than Optimism to Happiness. Surprise!

The cost of carelessness is way out
of proportion to the error it caused.

To make the world better, send children
out into it well taught to do the right thing.

"Professionals" take satisfaction in the work
itself, however others feel. Attitude is key.

A "professional" knows he succeeds when
he is respected by those he most respects.

Whatever one's potential, there is no
nobility in falling short. Keep stretching.

Fine distinctions and precise definitions
are essential conditions for clear thought.

Rejoice in the successes of others. Envy
is the enemy of your own contentment.

Arguments founded in principle, alas, are
unpersuasive to those who are unprincipled.

Excellence is a state-of-mind. State-of-mind
is a choice. By will alone, we can do better.

Ridicule and condemnation grow best in the
well fertilized soil of ignorant opposition.

Most live as embryonic chicks—within a
cramped shell, oblivious to wider reality.

At some point, acquiring more reduces
the value of what you have, leaving less.

Next to Love, what the child needs most is
Rational Consistency: parental predictability.

Wisdom is understanding the ever-
broadening consequence of any act.

Principles, like pearls, are carefully chosen,
matched & linked as part of a greater whole.

To purposely induce another to draw a
wrong inference is to deceive, i.e., to lie.

In things that count, settle for nothing short
of excellence. Excel where it counts most.

Live Love. In those two words, is the sum total of human wisdom for a happy life.

Even when lost, go straight. Any such path will lead somewhere. Wandering may not.

Judgment to be just must be truth-based, broad, balanced, and rational throughout.

War between Is and Ought always will be fought ... and always ought. Not for naught.

To praise and value some always excludes others who fall short. Discriminate justly.

To Think is to Be. Thus, to Think profoundly is to Be profoundly. Thin thought endangers.

Wisdom demands that you optimize your one life for happiness. That takes focus.

Enduring words on paper are more reliable than transient words spoke (merely wind).

Truly good managers either add value or they get out of the way of those who do!

Develop your sense of a distinct Self. Nonexistence is a truly poor option.

The mind is malleable—your slave or your tyrant, at your own choice. Take charge.

The simple man, judging a complex man, sees another simple man, never genius.

The simple man, judging a complex idea, sees a simple idea, rarely ingenuity.

The observable Law of Disproportionate Consequences inevitably prevails. Note.

Good decision-making begins with careful suspended judgment. Look before leaping.

A habit of making good habits beats deciding every issue on its own.

Savor every instant; the certain end hovers
but a fragile breath away for us all. Enjoy.

Fools all, acquisition our obsession over
Happiness. Really, how much is enough?

Past is past, irretrievable. Future is beyond
us, unknowable. Live now, while you can.

The "good life" is easier than we all think:
Right? do it. Wrong? don't. It's that simple.

Strive always to learn, to know, to try to
understand, to grow, to live. To truly be.

Every Self has an inalienable right to its own
Self … never to another's. Live true to you.

The question is never whether lines should
be drawn but where. Limits, too, have limits.

An idea can be both obvious and profound,
maybe so obvious its profundity is obscured.

Choose consciously to manage your mind. It is life's main tool. Spend attention with care.

In life, U-turns are rare. To choose the road is often to choose its end. No going back.

One cannot be all-accepting and all-inclusive and yet live by values. Values exclude some.

A team member who fails fails his team. The real challenge is, all of humanity is a team.

With love received comes the power to hurt the lover, imposing the solemn duty not to.

Ad libbing life is fraught with hazards for happiness. Principles help decide ahead.

Decide in advance who and what you will be. Then be that and not other than that.

The wisest ancients knew no shorter path to a life of abject misery than unwise love.

Expectation fathers Frustration, Impatience and Anxiety. But expectation bows to will.

Our best lies deep within us as potential yet unmined, like silver still in the mountain.

To receive also give: Respect. Empathy. Forgiveness. Appreciation. Mostly, Love.

Any change is sure to have unforeseeable ramifications. Big change=big consequence.

A thought half-thought does more damage than no thought at all. Think things through.

In public affairs, the price of Liberty is the key factor in every choice (often ignored).

Ultimately, every choice should be judged against its net good. Balance is ever the key.

Nothing is easier than impulsiveness … unless you count the bad consequences.

Strive to understand others, then fill in the gaps with Tolerance. A lotta good-will helps.

Admire the scholar's knowledge; yet never equate expertise with Truth. Or virtue.

One can learn a great deal about the wrong things. Beware overly impressive scholars.

To envy another of "higher class" is to assign Self to inferior station. Rank intimidates.

Once you conquer your Self, little else in life can defeat you. But Self is a formidable foe.

Retirement is an invitation to introspection and to discovery of new dimensions of Self.

Nothing stands between impulse and compulsion but Will. Will needs exercise.

Quicksilver Time teaches us to live every fleeting instant as it comes. Grasp this one!

When Impulse defeats Will, Conscience suffers and Will itself is weakened, again.

Necessity blinds morality. Equally so, perceived necessity, even more pernicious.

Impatience with slow change carries a high price indeed. Big change happens by degree.

Without Will, proclivities seek their default destiny in behavior. No control, no order.

Behavior, repeated, moves toward its default destiny—compulsion. Then chaos.

Be kind to the future you. Sooner you start, the kinder you'll be. In short, think long.

Change directions, but with prudence. Avoid high-speed turns. Turns can be hazardous.

Why squander fleeting moments when sublime ideas go ignored and unexamined?

Intellect is a talent, not a virtue. It merits admiration, not adulation. Character's more.

To make a monster, shield a child from consequences of his errant behavior.

No one ever succeeded at anything as just another head in the herd. Heed: Lead.

Emotion clouds Reason, Reason rules Will, Will controls Emotion. It's a closed loop.

For Reason to prevail, apply Will before Emotion gains control. Later is too late.

It is better to die usefully, young, than to only idly age, grousing and grumbling away.

Excess is the most destructive, and prevalent, of all human behaviors.

Life choices most alluring are, alas, often those most destructive. Book covers, tricky.

It is not only Right, it is Duty for each of us to be all that we can be. It's not all about us.

The most essential condition for maximum good is maximum liberty to pursue good.

Personal beauty is a gift which too often corrupts character. Beware. Danger lurks!

Each generation plants cultural time-bomb legacies to the future. Our errors outlive us.

To be subject to others' whim is slavery; to self-whim, self-slavery. Will breaks shackles.

Root out the root hate and all its resulting bitter fruit will wither away in due time.

To waste life: Be driven by impulse with disdain for consequences. Forecast: Failure!

The fault in those you disdain may lie not within them but within your own judgment.

Choose to think otherwise and rid yourself of your corrosive opinions. Think 'em gone.

The more decent one is, the more likely to expect decency in others. And vice versa.

Expectation of decency in others makes one vulnerable to indecent deception by others.

Those who trust are most likely trustworthy. Those not, not. Trusters make easy patsies.

Is there not a moral imperative to Optimize all we control? Waste not, especially talent.

For some, the future is not to be. Perhaps you, perhaps me. Live now! All is transient.

The villain in all prejudice is categorical thought, judging all by the worse examples.

The villain in all categorical thought is human nature. Complexity demands it.

Strive to excel; but expect resentment from those who choose not to. Envy is our nature.

———❖———

To succeed at anything, start with a model for excellence and strive to replicate that.

———❖———

Who we are is the sum of our habits. Our habits are the sum of our behavior. Alas!

———❖———

All worthy Principles are grounded in generalized Truth. Truth is a gift of God.

———❖———

Right choice requires right judgment on principles and particulars. Judge judiciously.

———❖———

The question is not "To be or not to be" but rather what to be. A choice. (Bard, fixed.)

———❖———

Talent is God's gift ... imposing duty of optimum use. Squandering talent is a sin.

———❖———

It is foolhardy to expect anything to act against its own nature. Man is no exception.

Rule for Life: Optimize all. Every choice, thought and act. Avoid waste and excess.

Thou Shalt Not Waste. That is a moral precept worthy of the stones of Moses.

Try to get to the root of all things. Seek out origins and fundamentals to clarify the rest.

Abdicate thought-escape as a way of life; thoughtlessness is, in a way, akin to Death.

Hate harms the hater. Even a hostile scorpion knows better than to sting himself.

There is an optimum sequence to do anything. It is a case of A before B, you C.

Start by defining the Ideal, then strive to get as close to it as you can at acceptable cost.

Hate hates the hater. Love loves the lover. Self-interest, too, counsels Love as a must.

Bad judgment is an incurable addiction.
Those afflicted with it inevitably suffer.

Sad truth is, there is no way, in the end, to protect people from their own bad choices.

Bad-choice insurance won't work; those who need it most would never think to buy it.

If it would harm all humanity for all to do it, don't do it. It's that simple. A good life rule.

What is higher Duty than the obligation of each part to the whole? Still, prioritize all.

"Victimless crime?" Clearly myth. Every crime against Self is a crime against all.

Every chip of the master's chisel is crucial to the sculpture's beauty. Chip carefully.

Every moral choice is crucial to the piecemeal formation of each Self.

Do what promotes the well-being of
Self without diminishing that of all.

Advanced education is not enough; one
must summon the will to strive to excel.

Pain has purpose. It teaches us all, and
disciplines us all, to strive to avoid harm.

No one is immune to consequences of his
errors and venality. Justice prevails. Good.

No loving parent, or God, would inoculate
his children from pain. Pain has purpose.

To write clearly, one must first think clearly.
Writing's the easy part. Learn. Think. Write.

The past and the future are entirely
different places. Extrapolation is chancy.

Life's larger lesson: It's not about you. It's
about the children. ALL about the children.

Male and female psyches are not contradictory but complementary.

We never graduate: Our obligation to posterity is enduring. It outlives us all.

Some add. Some subtract. Some are irrelevant. The choice, and duty, is ours.

"The Lost Generation" is unmitigated fiction. If only one generation is lost, ALL is lost.

One must choose before he can believe. Each must first choose what to believe.

To choose what to believe, think:
1) Thought. 2) Choice. 3) Belief.

Habit is the chisel with which we sculpt our Selves. Use Will skills to choose well.

Nonentity is no option. Identity is a first-order human need. Be authentically you.

Optimize! Optimize! Optimize! Always
balance gain, loss, and cost, then choose.

The lowly oyster has much to teach us
humans about dealing with irritants.

Faced with choice of uncertainties, the Wise
chose the one most likely. It's a "razor" idea.

Faced with choice of values, the Wise chose
the most likely virtuous. Another "razor."

Happiness is not a random quirk of fate.
Weighed right, it is the grand prize of life!

I have will power to do whatever I want,
but not enough, alas, to want what I should.

To be happy in an imperfect world, join Love
and Peace-of-Mind. Love is the easy part.

To optimize time spent, calculate Fluff-to-
Stuff Ratio (value density). Seek substance.

Consensus Principle: The broader the
weaker. More opinions weaken conclusions.

———⊶⊙⊶———

Whether it's me or you, this much is true:
there are lots of things we just don't do.

———⊶⊙⊶———

The trick is to carefully choose our never-do
things with purpose. Make a don't-do list.

———⊶⊙⊶———

Without habit, life's trivia would consume
our daily existence. Auto-pilots are needed.

———⊶⊙⊶———

Habit, clearly, is a great liberating gift of
God if wisely used as a tool, not a tyrant.

———⊶⊙⊶———

Choose habits aware that the choice is to be
either free or enslaved. Shuck your shackles.

———⊶⊙⊶———

To do wrong and feel no guilt is a double sin.
The second is ever the most grievous by far.

———⊶⊙⊶———

Pleasure can result from right or wrong.
Happiness is ever right. They differ nuch.

Everything is desired for purpose with higher purpose—all except Happiness.

All that unites us with some divides us from others. Unity is forever elusive, alas!

The beast knows neither Right nor Wrong. Only Man must choose, the burden all his.

If an idea be part lie, it ultimately becomes all lie. The lie leaches through all it touches.

All that is is forever altered by all that happens. Each instant is new, yet older.

We live on, and on again, in consequences long after memories and records perish.

Effects ripple onward. Consider the duty we owe humanity to get it right the first time.

No one is more gullible than a completely honest person. Knaves make lousy patsies.

It is harsh truth that, at some point (except for the noblest) Threat trumps Principle.

Say what you mean, exactly what you mean. Brevity is laudable but Clarity is paramount.

Most of the fault in any communication is fault of the communicator, less the receiver.

How precious is a Life? Now, how precious is any moment of Life? Cherish every second.

Teaching is the noblest calling of all. All our tomorrows depend upon children learning.

A tree that blossoms but bears no fruit is beautiful, but all pretense. Outcomes rule.

Live this very day a life of joy. A long winter's night awaits us all. All too soon ...

Reality, being commonplace, is mundane. But it is where most of us live out our lives.

Live each day in the light of Right; there'll be darkness enough for all when night falls.

Giving more, you become more. Becoming more, you give more—a closed loop system.

Trust Reason, the servant. Beware of Emotion, the tyrant. To be free: reason.

Fashion and Fad are herd habits. Your choices are your responsibility alone.

All living things are content within their natural lot. Except discontented humanity.

Contentment is denied Man alone. With more, he wants more. Ain't no satisfaction!

However wise, there's no better advice than this: Be prudent always in all things.

There is but one addiction: self-indulgence. Alas, there is only one cure: self-restraint.

Learn to conquer the moment and the long-term will take care of itself. It is never easy.

With sufficient time to live, we have it within us to rise to our potential. Tragically, few do.

Falling short is failure of Will, Wisdom or Love. Rarely Ability. Will only is a choice.

One of life's hardest lessons is to learn to pick the important things. (Trivia is a trap.)

Most of us burn up our lives on trivialities and banalities, neglecting the best within us.

One's conclusions and assumptions change over a lifetime. At least, they ought to.

Every scar on the Soul mars one's potential for Happiness. Soul wounds are avoidable.

Summon the will to pick up a difficult book and read it through. Train yourself to dig.

Neglect of education traps us in a little
cosmos, dwarfed by our own ignorance.

Wisdom expands the breadth of our horizons
and the clarity of our most distant vision.

The price of self-indulgence is a little life.
Learn to live large. Cultivate your own mind.

Life void of coherence and meaning is empty
and ultimately joyless. Seek out substance.

The fatal mistake in most folly is the
assumption of a rare best-case outcome.

Only greater purpose can liberate us from
the tyranny of the moment's temptations.

Cherish all that is True, Beautiful, and Good.
To live the best strive to detest the rest.

We are puppets manipulated by the ideas of
others. Choose your puppeteers with care.

To use logic on a fool is to pick the wrong tool. A trick or a threat is a far better bet.

———◦∞◦———

All things good in moderation become horrid in excess! All impulses gravitate to excess.

———◦∞◦———

Are you victimized? By a hostile, unfair world, or by your own choice of mindset?

———◦∞◦———

If nothing is Right, then nothing is Wrong and all is permitted at no cost to the Good.

———◦∞◦———

It is, alas, a truism that the acts of the worst of us reflect on the best of us. It's a given.

———◦∞◦———

It is a moral duty for all of us to condemn the bad in the worst of us. Ours IS to judge.

———◦∞◦———

In sports, business, war, and most of life itself—the decisive factor is the will to win.

———◦∞◦———

In all forms of competition, one must summon the drive to strive. Lagers lose.

Excellence is excellent but, alas, necessarily exceptional. The ordinary is more popular.

Judgment, like stew, is best savored after given time to settle and blend. Haste hurts.

The longer you follow the wrong path, the more lost you become. Wandering is waste.

First thoughts are more often wrong than right. Think again, think it through & choose.

Study the Great in any domain and you'll find they all stand in shifting sand, mortal.

Extravagance is just another form of Waste. Duty calls for Prudence. Excess is an enemy.

"Doubt grows with knowledge." (Goethe) … certainty, with youth and ignorance.

The locus of life is the mind. To live large, expand the mind. Learn lots and keep at it.

What I know to be true is to Truth as one mustard seed is to the limitless cosmos.

The timeless ideas of great thinkers inspire, nourish and humble the hungry mind.

Cherish each new insight as a "delicious awakening." (quote: Ralph Waldo Emerson)

There is no new truth, merely newly perceived truth. True Truth is durable truth.

One must be diligently blind to avoid questioning his own entrenched ideas.

Of what value is reason in the face of adamant dogmatism? It is futile there.

The tragic truth about Truth is it is Desire, not evidence, which too often prevails.

Placebos work. The mind often triumphs over reality to make its own flawed truth.

Each new insight is a bright beacon that illuminates lasting future understanding.

Truth has many homes. It resides in neither age nor sage nor ideology. It is where it is.

Indifference to durable Truth is humanity's unsurpassed folly. Always at tragic cost.

When fads fever the collective mind, Reason abandons us. Like herds, we may stampede.

Philosophy is synthesizing truth through insight into experience, precisely expressed.

History speaks this clearly: the human capacity to endure is elastic. Thank God.

The seeds of Wisdom take firm root when one first savors the sweet joys of Clarity.

Each mind is condemned by fate's design to dwell in its own time. Context alters all.

Passion is a fire which, when beyond our control, consumes reason. Passion is easier.

———⊷∞⊷———

All knowledge is fragmentary; all resulting conclusions, are therefore deeply suspect.

———⊷∞⊷———

Without Truth, Reason is lost. Without Reason, Truth is unfound. The link is lasting.

———⊷∞⊷———

Only fools look to a mind ruled by passion for logical inferences. Passion blinds Truth.

———⊷∞⊷———

All argument is advocacy, therefore inevitably selective. Thus, less than Truth.

———⊷∞⊷———

Be wary. Hunger-to-believe can be a treacherous enemy of Truth. Bias blinds.

———⊷∞⊷———

Wisdom eludes those without reverence for it. Like Virtue. Like Honor. Like Truth itself.

———⊷∞⊷———

Words are but wind. It is their meanings which have meaning. Look deeper, always.

Could there be a more egregious lie than a lie to oneself about oneself? Be true to you.

Fine distinction is the essence of clear thought. Think, speak and write precisely.

Wrong ideas wreck lives … and alter the destiny of nations. Believe with great care.

Artists reject rules; for them, the purpose of art is its own unrestrained perfection.

Omniscience is God's alone … the rest of us view selective reality and think it is Truth.

Universals are not, nor can they ever be, the creation of Man. They are God's realm only.

All that has been, is, and all that continues is part of what will be. All that is consequence.

With so much that is unknown, is there any way not to be, in some degree, wrong?

Man's most pernicious affliction is ignorance of his own ignorance. Knowledge is the cure.

Words heard are never what is said. Thoughts written, never what is read.

Without grasp of the past, life shrinks to the breath of the moment. Amnesia's a threat.

There are few greater joys than the joy of Understanding. There's never enough of it.

Any idea, like a falling staged domino, has consequences which have consequences.

From Knowledge, Insight ... Insight, Wisdom ... Wisdom, Clarity ... Clarity, right choice.

There is no lesson so worth learning—or teaching—as self-control. All begins there.

Without Truth, there can be no Honor ... or Justice ... or Trust. Truth is the cornerstone.

All perceived truth is subjective. All Truth, however, is objective. The latter's God only.

Reality is a kaleidoscope in perpetual flux. Expect no reruns. Each tick of time is new.

I understand that the understanding I crave is ever elusive. Knowing is ever incomplete.

Each mind is unique, not only in data content, in processes as well. No duplicates.

We are God's creations, details sculpted by the uncertain hand of our own inept past.

One must learn in order to know, know in order to understand … then still fall short.

Today, nothing is so free, so accessible and so valuable as Knowledge … nothing but air.

History is what it is—Truth—whatever writers do to distort it to their purposes.

Consequences ripple ever outward in concentric circles from every act, on and on.

One can lead any willing fool to the well of knowledge, but never make him think.

Expect no objectivity from a partisan. Alas, in the end, we are all partisans, it seems.

From a single seedling idea a forest of thoughts may ultimately grow and flourish.

Each Self is singular, unique across all of humanity for all of time, irreplaceable.

Born in another time, my life could be more like my father's than mine. I prefer mine.

Insight is the sudden convergence of ideas seemingly unrelated, unwilled, purposeful.

Philosophy, in essence, is the search for essence. Look deeply to origins of things.

Those who prefer illusion to Truth remain voluntarily blind to realities of living well.

He who is ignorant of his own ignorance remains irredeemably ignorant, sadly lost.

A new insight is a new awakening! And you will never again be as shallow as you were.

Beware of the seedling idea. One never knows how or where a forest will grow.

Inadequacy of evidence is no hindrance to the simple mind, but then expect no justice.

Confront your contradictions. In a perfect philosophy, all the pieces fit like a puzzle.

Insight, it seems, is beyond will. It appears to possess a will of its own. Why is that?

Ignorance is baneful; indifference to Ignorance, clearly, is far more pernicious.

Sophistication lies in the eyes of the unsophisticated. To others, it is a given.

Myth, metaphor, proverb or fact, Truth is never diminished by its conveyance.

All Truth is compatible, never contradictory. One could label this "The Unity of Truth."

Faced with choice of certain uncertainties, the Wise choose the one most likely as best.

Faced with choice of values, the Wise choose the one most likely virtuous as best option.

The sum of history is not the work of knaves and fools. Knaves and fools only subtract.

I not only don't know what I don't know, I don't even know what I know … I think!

The more one learns, the more one learns there remains vastly more yet to learn.

The troubling truth is, it is what is believed that is at issue, not merely what is asserted.

One cannot justly judge a man long dead whose history is written by his enemies.

Truth and Wisdom share this: both are rare and being rare, are too rarely recognized.

Be wary of building your conclusions upon the conclusions of others. Hazards lurk.

Preoccupied, sadly, while rare Truths float past, ignored, like transient cloud images.

The leisure of retirement is an invitation to introspection and discovery of one's Self.

It is not so much facts that divide us as our interpretation of facts and goals that vary.

Without Truth as a standard, all is permitted … and nothing can be truly believed.

Only Truth separates us from barbarism, chaos, error and the idiocy of philosophers.

What of Faith and Doubt? Though ever at odds, both are essential to the Truth-seeker.

To seek Truth requires Faith that Truth exists and is worthy of pursuit. Faith is key & first.

To be ignorant is, in a way, to be dead. Living is knowing. Knowing means seeking.

The mortal mind exhibits a seemingly unlimited capacity for oversimplification.

In a world of fools, one values no opinion incompatible with his own. Thus fools win.

Whether scoundrels or knaves, nobles or saints, genius is genius, admirable or not.

Each newborn comes equipped with an equal supply of ignorance. Progress varies.

There is a kind of beauty still in a tightly reasoned, densely supported argument.

Wrong ideas spring up like weeds from the rocky soil of unattended minds. Best pulled.

Truth is often messy, a hodgepodge of contradictions and apparent irrelevancies.

The bias of any storyteller is the story itself. One might call that inevitability "Story Bias."

Simplified, any story is something other than Truth, a sales pitch, at best, partial truth.

All that I think, all that I am is rooted in all that I have learned and felt and been.

Try as I might, I can imagine no more than a fragment of Truth. The rest may refute it all.

Like fish in a pond, we all swim in a tiny pool of our own unique circumstance: "Reality."

Every conclusion is a generalization—a synthesis of conflicting complexities.

All generalizations are oversimplifications, something other than reality, and flawed.

Multitudes sleepwalk through a king's garden of insight's blooming delights.

As I am, so I think. As I think, so I am. It is a closed-loop system, but expandable, I think.

We can never know completely. Not any thing. We can know, at best, but partially.

We can approach Truth but not possess it in its entirety. Perceived Truth is fragmentary.

Alas, in the final analysis, we are all merely abject prisoners of the thoughts of others.

Beware. The mind is a sometimes duplicitous friend. Maybe worse. Think again if you can.

There is no higher calling for the intellect than the pursuit of Truth, tho ever elusive.

All living things have this key advantage over Man: they are incapable of irrationality.

What one believes to be Truth is the anchor of life. Without belief, we are adrift, lost.

Those unwilling not to lie are untrustworthy to believe. Truth makes cowards of us all.

No one thinks alone. Every thinker has his sources. The wise choose sources carefully.

Those with no reverence for Truth logically have no moral compunction against lying.

Why grant an ounce of credence to those relativists who assert, "There is no Truth!"?

Wit, too, is insight—born of spontaneous, reflexive connection of disparate particulars.

With wit, timeliness is critical—its wit's
worth withering quickly past its moment.

———✦———

When Truth is out of reach, settle for
Common Sense. Choose what's likely so.

———✦———

To understand what men truly believe,
examine their actions. Acts seldom lie.

———✦———

Perceived truth varies among perceivers but
Objective Truth simply is what it always is.

———✦———

This irresistible urge within that drives us to
seek the essence of all—a "Seeking Sense."

———✦———

Every evil that men do is the unavoidable
cost consequence of humanity's Free Will.

———✦———

Within all creatures, there is a common inner
beauty. Seek that always, not its opposite.

———✦———

Nothing is trivial, nothing contrary to the
ultimate Greater Good. Not even Evil itself.

All living things share in the overpowering desire to live free … and live to the fullest.

"Thou shalt live." "Thou shalt be free." Unstated commandments Moses missed.

Every single thing in the universe is unique; purposeful diversity is pervasive throughout.

Past is past. Present soon done. The future? Ah! All is Potential there! It's where life is.

Potential pulses within the precious egg; a majestic eagle there awaits its time to soar.

Potential is as sacred as Life itself; they are separated by time alone. It is what life is.

David preexisted in the unquarried marble, awaiting Michelangelo's certain hand.

It is imperative for each living thing to strive toward its own well-being! Duty calls us all.

Is it not the obligation of each to all for every talent to perform at its limits? Waste is sin.

———

Despair not. Man has come a long way since dawn, and it is yet early morning. Patience.

———

This prodding voice within that whispers lofty thoughts—can it be but a nobler me?

———

The truth about Truth is that it is Desire, not evidence, which too often prevails.

———

Truth has its own hierarchy. There are higher truths & lower truths and shades between.

———

No Hope, no Joy. Thus, atheism offers only a bleak path to a dark polar night. Emptiness.

———

Since dawn, humankind has shared a universal yearning to know the Unknowable.

———

Placebos work. The mind often triumphs over reality to make its own truth.

It is far better to have lived and died than never to have lived at all. Cry not for cows.

———⊷⊙⊶———

Surely every law of the universe is essential to all others & their shared grand purpose.

———⊷⊙⊶———

In spite of all its infinite complexity, the universe works! Nothing by Man compares.

———⊷⊙⊶———

Science, Religion, and Philosophy all revolve around a common axis: understanding God.

———⊷⊙⊶———

Human understanding creeps inexorably toward ever deeper grasp of most things.

———⊷⊙⊶———

The assumption in every argument, every credo, is that all alternatives are wrong.

———⊷⊙⊶———

Reason is Man's unique master blessing. Clearly, we were meant to use it. Think.

———⊷⊙⊶———

Whence came this insight? From marvels of my mind? Surely. But whence came those?

There's so much that's unknowable—ever. It staggers and humbles the puny mind.

———⸻———

A "universal" is derived from discovering commonalties among particulars of a class.

———⸻———

The hen pecks her egg while the chick taps from within. Truth cracks through to light.

———⸻———

Similarly, when Mind asks and Soul answers in perfect resonance, understanding is born.

———⸻———

Wonder why the unhatched chick pecks at its shell to discover a new world unknown?

———⸻———

Within its very nature the unhatched chick may possess a Seeking Sense akin to Faith.

———⸻———

Though it is not for mortal minds to grasp Why? there is surely purpose to all that is.

———⸻———

Even in the face of suffering, we can rest assured there is a benevolent logic to all.

It's axiomatic: the broader the consensus, the weaker its principles ... and vice versa.

I conclude there can be happiness only where love is accompanied by mind peace.

Critical to the formula for Happiness are Joy and Hope which rest on Belief and Faith.

Each of us has within potentials beyond the reach of our wildest imagination. Keep at it.

The key to discovering one's potentials is first to have faith that they indeed exist.

Potential unsought too often remains unfound. Faith precedes discovery.

To the abandoned weak calf, God seems cruel. To the healthier herd, God is love.

The calf's sad loss was Destiny, the certain consequence of Things-The-Way-They-Are.

Things-The-Way-They-Are is good. Even,
ultimately, for the abandoned weak calf.

With reason and will and moral sense, we
have what we need to deal with life's trials.

Show me a troubled heart and I'll show you
a seeking soul yet unsettled. Seek anyway.

Competing orthodoxies have ever grappled
with varied visions of the same high Truths.

Truth vs Justice? Truth, clearly, for Truth
exists without Justice, never the opposite.

Daunting dare: Try to imagine a better world
than one in which Love ruled every heart.

Truth is absolute. My perceptions of Truth
are varying, tentative and often wrong.

Whatever is, must be—the sum of the vast
interplay between Cause and Consequence.

Cosmic order masquerades as chaos for those without faith. Order ever prevails.

In this purposeful universe, there is no Chance; only endless Consequence.

I trim and I trim but the manicured yaupon holly in my yard refuses to be enslaved.

My holly inspires me with its lasting lust to live free, according to its God-given nature.

Because Order is universal, atheism is the least plausible of all belief systems.

Through Reason alone, it is clear that Love is the Ultimate and Happiness, its outcome.

Is it not the obligation of talent to perform at its limits? To waste talent is surely sin.

All is consequence, from Original Cause to Infinity, with each effect still another cause.

With justice done, all the grievous things I
didn't do should help balance out my tally.

God's own law prevails everywhere, always,
universally. That could be The Law of Laws.

The basis for Knowledge is Faith—faith that
Truth exists and has value worthy of pursuit.

In that light, all enlightenment, it would
seem, of necessity, begins with Faith.

Welfare of the herd eclipses that of the calf.
This is still another of God's universal laws.

Observation, experience, common sense
& faith in purpose reveal gobs about God.

Nothing is ephemeral; all of existence is an
unbroken continuum of cause and effect.

If God is indeed in some measure within
each of us, how must we treat all others?

Judgment is not ours to render; so be gentle in what you believe about beliefs of others.

God deals from his deck of Potentials. It is for us to play each hand as best we can.

What seems flawed now is surely ideal in the context of eternity. All is purposeful there.

God is Love. God is Reason. In those six words lies the essence of ultimate Truth.

Disbelief is no less a belief system than any other. It should not be forced upon others.

Who am I, merely mortal, to presume to embrace the truth I find? Still, I must try.

Like it or not, destruction of the Old is a necessary sacrifice to birth of the New.

I don't think I know. But I can't know that I don't know. I may very well know but not.

Omniscience belongs to God alone. Mortals view a selective, biased reality. A mirage.

The mere existence of universals is sufficient evidence of God to refute all atheists.

Who am I to harbor such passions for the world to conform to my own flawed design?

Without Faith, there is no Hope; without Hope, no Faith. Without Truth, neither.

Truth is Truth as surely as Gold is Gold. The Treasure is not limited by where it is found.

Without innate longing for God, Earth's all would be left to perish by our greedy hand.

Each living thing is compelled by its design to express its nature. In this, truly we are one.

Ongoing renewal is the theme of all living things—the source of progress and hope.

An inborn seeking sense, shared like the air, inspires a need for meaning in every heart.

Each of us is but one stage—an essential stage—in God's endless process of renewal.

All of life, clearly, is a continuum, an ongoing process, progressing according to a Plan.

Each hour, advancing the Plan, is thus better than the hours that preceded it. Have faith.

If Happiness were universal, inevitable, easy or cheap, it would surely lose its worth.

All possibilities are part of God's creation; all impossibilities are imposed by His limits.

Imagine a world in which the irritant that plagues you did not exist to find its purpose.

God has given us the main tools. It's up to us to strive to realize our own full potential.

Unified theory of God and the Universe:
Where there is design, there is a designer.

Within David there is surely something of
Michelangelo; Made and Maker are as one.

We are unique creations from God's clay,
sculpted by our own uncertain hand.

There is no belief so rational as belief in a
rational universe created with rationality.

Pervasive rationality suggests that even
irrationality oddly has rational purpose.

All that is is meant to be—for a reason. God
is capable of everything, except irrationality.

Cosmic Logic must hold reason for all things.
Otherwise, as I see it, what is would not be.

I write down these thoughts as they occur
—because I can. And, because I can, I must.

Each of God's gifts of talent is unique and purposeful. It is our duty to do our best.

Whatever I can do can nowhere be exactly duplicated. If it is to be done, I must do it.

Any talent, great or small, carries with it the obligation for its expression. Its use is duty.

Without some human intuition of a core Truth at the heart of all, Man is adrift.

It is to the Greater Good (and each of its parts) that we, as parts, are morally bound.

Seeking God through Reason is evidence of reason-grounded Faith that God exists.

Envision the Sum-of-All. Surely only One greater than All-That-Is could be its Creator.

Skeptics who feel faith without proof is the folly of fools should reflect on raw instinct.

The chick within its imprisoning egg needs no proof of a larger life in order to seek it.

The best reason to do anything is that it will result in The Greater Good, God's clear goal.

The soil within which each religion grows best is the culture from which it arises.

Each religion grows out of distinct cultural differences to form its own pathway to God.

Each belief system must stake exclusive claim on The Correct Path. All else is not.

To live. To live happy. To live free to seek happiness. These are Life's 1st imperatives.

Consensus is ephemeral. Like all life-based things, belief systems must adapt or die.

Without beliefs, chaos reigns ... leaving us lost in a maelstrom of competing ideals.

There is a sublime unity throughout all life, uninterrupted from conception to death.

Negative expectations are incompatible with Christian ideals. Christianity inspires hope.

All of God's gifts have purpose, though they may be used, and misused, at will's whim.

Pursue Happiness by discerning the nature of First Intent, then, align desires with that.

The rational mind favors the Greater Good. Other choices, by definition, are irrational.

The Greater Good surely will be always congenial with God's ultimate purpose.

Unified Theory of Everything: God's purpose surely is the Greater Good for All-That-Is.

Truly, the seed of a rose yet to blossom is of equal worth with the flower at full bloom.

All Truth is compatible. All the pieces fit. One could rightly label this "The Unity of Truth."

A mere mite in an immense dark cosmos, I can somehow embrace All. Even God.

All choices should be judged against a single standard: net effect on The Greater Good.

Not just life but abundant life—the survival imperative embraces all. Strive to flourish.

In a rational universe, what is needed is provided. And all provided is needed.

Only Truth separates us from barbarism, chaos and the idiocy of philosophers.

What is it that links Faith with Doubt? Both are essential to the Truth-seeker's quest.

To seek Truth requires that one have Faith that Truth exists and is worthy of pursuit.

Doubt shields the Truth-seeker from much grievous error. Truth has strict standards.

Like a knife, Reason has great and varied utility--for good or evil and shades between.

Man alone among living things shares in the pervasive rationality that rules the universe.

Man stands far above all other living things as a reflection of his Creator's rationality.

No object of Creation has Man's ability to perceive his relationship with All-That-Is.

Man alone is empowered to glimpse his own significance & be awed by his insignificance.

It is not only Right, it is Duty, for each of us to be all that we can be. That's best for all.

The essential condition for Man is the freedom to pursue his full potential.

Within every acorn lurks a mighty oak, given opportunity to grow. Life is all potential.

Reason is depicted as cold. In truth, there is inspiring Beauty in Reason, a first-order gift.

Rationality is Man's gift alone to conceive of a rational universe with a rational Creator.

The Creator of All-That-Is permeates All-That-Is and thus each that is. Even me!

Evil, it seems, is like a pervasive deadly virus which thrives only in receptive human hosts.

Should all of humanity perish leaving the rest of All-That-Is, Evil would become extinct.

Ethos dies. Always slowly, but ultimately, through atrophy ... and at tragic cost.

The wisdom of the ancient wise inspires awe even in contrast with our wisest moderns.

Thoughts we thought were original have
been thought long before by wiser others.

———◦◦◦———

The Soul seems the sum of Self, even the
animating spirit that inspires Man to Truth.

———◦◦◦———

It's not white whiskers but Reason, Love and
divine Purpose which God shares with Man.

———◦◦◦———

Universals are beyond the capability of Man.
Thus, they are the exclusive domain of God.

———◦◦◦———

Man alone among all living creatures can
perceive and recognize God's universals.

———◦◦◦———

Why does all this exist? Surely Reason
grounded in Purpose is the rational answer.

———◦◦◦———

If there is Purpose, we reason, surely from
the sum of all we see, that Purpose is Good.

———◦◦◦———

In the design rules for the universe,
everything is optimized for the Good.

Without morality, no virtue. Without virtue, Man, by far, is most beastly of all the beasts.

All living things have this key advantage over humans: they are incapable of irrationality.

We stand at the mouth of our cave, club in hand, ready to defend the helpless within.

The absence of explanation does not mean there is no reason, only none we may know.

Is there not some moral imperative to Optimize all over which we have influence?

Each mind is the unique sum of its own biology and experience. No two are alike.

If all that's needed is provided and all provided, needed, then to optimize is duty.

Waste of any ilk is not only wasteful but wrong. That's my case for optimizing all.

Even in the most despicable of non-human creatures one cannot find an iota of evil.

Life is either meaningless or it isn't. If you think it is, it is. Meaning's key to happiness.

The ability of the mind to derive general truths is a talent independent of all learned.

For self-destructive behavior, there are no "victimless crimes." The Self suffers, too.

Every crime against Self is a crime against humanity. In the end, any crime hurts us all.

To observe the Effect—existence—and then to deny an adequate Cause is abject folly.

Reason alone, uninformed by innate sense of right & wrong, is a poor arbiter of Truth.

What is politics if not reciprocal favoritism? And what is that if not abject corruption?

It is the moral duty of each generation to improve the well-being of all who follow.

Every chip of the master's chisel is crucial to the sculpture's lasting beauty. Chip carefully.

Thus it is with each crisis of moral choice in the piecemeal formation of every Self.

God could readily decree good behavior of all ... if he preferred puppets to humans.

Disbelief is also a belief system as is belief that one cannot know what to believe.

Knowledge and intellect, akin to tools and skills, are not ends but means—enablers.

To assess the value of anything, imagine the universe without it. Conflict, for example.

When proof proves elusive, settle for your next best rationally compelling Reason.

History's progress is the sum of man's
wisdom minus his folly—the net result.

Be afraid of media's masters lest they
become your own. Shape your own mind.

To believe what one cannot know requires
reason, faith and desire. Truth is the goal.

Every story is biased by its teller; every
perception is biased by its perceiver.

Every social system is stratified. The key is
how freely individuals move up and down.

Every confusing complexity contains within
itself a simple Truth. Find that core Truth.

The art of Wisdom is the distillation
of complexity to its simplest essence.

Life's larger lesson: It's not about you. It's
about the children, all about the children.

All that is is forever altered by all that happens. Nothing is without consequence.

———◦∞◦———

A wish for others who wish for others: A long life, good health, happiness and an easy exit.

———◦∞◦———

If to resist power is "reactionary," then, worse, to impose it must be "actionary."

———◦∞◦———

We live on in consequences long after any memory or record of our brief existence.

———◦∞◦———

Consider, the weighty moral obligation we owe humanity to get it right the first time.

———◦∞◦———

No faith, no hope. No hope, no progress toward a better life. Belief is first essential.

———◦∞◦———

For the Good, may these prevail: 1) Truth, 2) Love, 3) Liberty, 4) Justice. All in order.

———◦∞◦———

Truth is first, for without it, the values that follow fail. Likewise Love, Liberty, & Justice.

All that we are. All that we are capable of becoming is first designed in as Potential.

All life's potential resides in the seed. The acorn + time is an oak, if allowed to thrive.

An endless war rages between Want and Will in endless contention over Is vs. Ought.

What Man has made is easily recognized by its flaws, inconsistencies, and imperfections.

Whatever is left, lacking flaws from the hand of Man, can only be the ideal work of God.

Leaves fall to nourish the tree. What may seem flawed is, in truth, often perfection.

To believe in God and not cherish Truth is a contradiction. The reverse is equally true.

Multitudes search in vain for Meaning, never sensing that everything is meaningful.

There is nothing quite so prevalent in human beliefs as contradiction. Try to resolve yours.

Scarcity & plenty, pain & suffering, life & death, good & evil. All this is purposeful.

Happiness doesn't result from living right. But living right vastly improves its chances.

Human hunger for Meaning is universal. Universality reveals purposeful design.

All that is is the grand synthesis of all that has been. Each moment is a new synthesis.

Potential is the great promise from God for all we are capable of becoming, if we will it.

Those proclaiming most tolerance seem least tolerant of views opposing their own.

Without Truth, there is no basis for morality. Without morality, there is no sin or guilt.

Without sin or guilt, there's no conscience.
Without conscience, all lawful is allowed.

No deep Truth of God is diminished one tittle by our quibbling over details of dogma.

All things are connected. How so is the pursuit of philosophy, science and religion?

Every scar on the Soul mars Happiness. Scar tissue lacks sensitivity ... and is always ugly.

Every Ethos falls victim to acceptance of divergent ideas. Thus, Ethos atrophies.

Detached philosophical observation is less heated and more persuasive than debate.

Life void of all meaning, with no sense of larger purpose, is ultimately starved for Joy.

Order and stability are ever transient. Beliefs and Customs provide essential coherence.

Competing Beliefs and Customs conflict.
Competition is pervasive through nature.

To understand the behavior of any living
thing, look to its nature. Scorpion's sting.

The driving impulse of all life is not only to
survive but to flourish, to exist insufficient.

If God is not, all is chaos from mere random
happenstance, without purpose or meaning.

If God is, he could have chosen otherwise but
didn't. So, All-That-Is is just as he has chosen

Who are we, mere mites, to find fault with
All-That-Is and petition for dispensation?

Nothing else in the vast cosmos has minute
Man's awesome, exclusive power of Reason.

With Reason, Man alone senses his own
relevance and significance in God's scheme.

Vast empty space, endless time and lifeless rock is not God's masterwork. Man clearly is.

We're learning to tolerate all our differences—save one: difference in thought and belief.

Human Progress ends here: In matters of ideas and beliefs, we remain irreconcilable.

Drop a rock and it falls. That's a universal truth, a law of nature—clearly a "miracle."

There are those who "know" and the wise who recognize how much they do not know.

"Why me, Lord!" I wail. "Why not you?" whispers the troubling answer in my mind.

It's ironic but it seems everything tends to give meaning and value to its opposite.

Progress, by all means, but with prudence. Reckless impatience comes at high costs.

Yes, there is evil within us all. But there is goodness as well. And therein lies all hope.

Culture provides the cohesion essential for a collaborative society. Shared beliefs are key.

The striving of primal Man to understand was not "superstition" but Reason's seed.

Truth is Truth, just as gold is gold; its value is intrinsic. Where it is found matters not.

We disagree. So you think I must have been fooled while what others told you was true?

Where we disagree, it may be that we value different things or the same in mere degree.

Nothing that is in nature is without cause, consequence, and purpose. Lots else ain't!

Each wrong choice has its ultimate cost and each right choice has its ultimate reward.

General Truth, itself, is God's gift as is the uniquely human ability to perceive it.

Relish this moment; the next may not be so pleasant ... or, for you, come to pass at all!

Peace-of-Mind, second only to Love for Happiness = Hope + Equanimity with All.

Hope, in turn = Trust in God's Purpose + Faith in God's Benevolence (i.e., Love).

People resent those whose benevolence makes them feel needy and dependent.

To avoid feeling needy & dependent, some consider the generosity shown them a right.

Love is everything, and everything without love is nothing. (Diderot paraphrased)

To be content with an imperfect world is a sentiment unworthy of the noble heart.

To discard history's gains in the name of
Progress may be a crime against civilization.

———◦∞◦———

Love is Heaven. Hate is Hell. Purgatory
is a barren land in between called Apathy.

———◦∞◦———

The great ideas of past genius inspire,
nourish and humble the hungry mind.

———◦∞◦———

He who steals the peace from my mind
steals my happiness, a grievous offense.

———◦∞◦———

He who steals my happiness steals the
essence of my life. It is akin to murder.

———◦∞◦———

The radius of trust ever expands among
humanity, inevitable turbulence at its edge.

———◦∞◦———

Without Trust, there is no Love, no Peace-
of-Mind, no Happiness. Trust rests on Truth.

———◦∞◦———

To behold a stunning sunset ever inspires a
mystical resonance in the receptive heart.

Awe and Beauty cannot account for the
sunset's wonder. It is God's giving touch.

That ineffable bond we feel with nature
is surely the unifying touch of its Creator.

Style often seems the polar opposite of
Substance. But, instead, it is its mirror.

Style—including avoidance of style—speaks
volumes about the substance of that within.

Aside from Love, nothing is more essential
to Happiness than mind peace (a choice).

All creatures share a common inner beauty
that surpasses all outward difference.

Peacock and warthog are, after all,
masterworks of the same Creator.

Tradition, distilled best past practices,
binds old and new to common purpose.

Any feat of ability at its peak reveals a
glimpse of the ideal of human potential.

———

Happiness is no random quirk of fate. It is
the grand prize of life! Ultimately a choice.

———

Happiness happens ... if you give enough of
yourself to make it happen. Thus it's earned.

———

With each new wrinkle comes broader
wisdom, deeper faith, and greater love.

———

Age brings manifold, deeper gifts beyond the
shallow imagination of the evolving young.

———

High culture is a wall elites use to separate
themselves as superior to the multitudes.

———

Fine arts are weapons of the upper order
wielded to keep philistines from their gates.

———

Ecstasy-of-Insight and Love-of-Truth are
inseparable parts of the same sweet whole.

This voice within—can it be but a nobler me?
Or is it something mysteriously more?

Whose voice is it that whispers these lofty
thoughts in my solitary reflections? Mine?

It is a paradox that Happiness is nourished
far more by outlook than circumstance.

Happiness lies within the grasp of those who
will but seize it. Determination trumps fate.

Think: Are not our greatest blessings made
even more precious by their opposites?

Would Light have meaning without Dark?
Good without Bad? Life without Death?

Take heart: with each disappointment, the
odds for improvement improve. Statistically.

Whatever we have in this life is worth only
the value we give it. Everything, even Love.

Family is truly a great gift, for those blessed with the wisdom to recognize that this is so.

The creative impulse defies repression. It cannot be enslaved but may be indentured.

Those who cherish ideas over material wealth are more certain to die enriched.

The avant-garde earnestly strive to set themselves apart from the plodding herd.

Nature's wonder inspires in us feelings of helplessness, insignificance, stunned awe.

Is it truth (or mere hubris) that the most wondrous creation of all is humanity itself?

The impulse to advance Well-being is second only to Survival in all living things. So strive.

In the human species, alone, "Well-being" ultimately translates as "Happiness."

Happiness depends on Joy and Hope which, in turn, rest entirely on Belief and Faith.

If it is morally wrong to harm others, it is arguably equally wrong to harm oneself.

Deprivation of happiness constitutes a principal harm--the theft of life's essence.

Those devoid of interest are deprived of the excitement & joy of mind-expanding insight.

Ultimately, every act is selfish, including charity, self-sacrifice and moral behavior.

As the hours slip by, senses seem to sharpen. It is as if they wisely know it will soon be dark.

Old and young differ on the relative value placed upon both excitement and serenity.

Restraint is the essence of all art ... and behavior ... and public policy ... and far more.

In the choices of my life, unchallenged command is in the firm hand of Captain Me.

Inside, below, though, there's a nobler deck hand who aspires in vain for a turn at helm.

Like a rock, Love is ever there, standing steadfast against eroding surf tides of time.

He who is at peace within accepts with equanimity all that comes with living life.

Undisturbed by insight, many drift aimlessly about while their destiny forms unnoticed.

An inspiration of thought, an entirely new insight, leaps to life in joy, unsummoned.

Insight is akin to giving birth without pain to an infant with unlimited potential over time.

Shields of Emotion, when sufficiently strong, can blunt spears of Reason, however sharp.

The strong ropes that bind us are woven
from the thin twine of shared daily trivia.

The artistic mind is in touch with the soul.
Feelings rule all art. Reason wilts before it.

Those who lead with their right brain seldom
gravitate to rule-based pursuits. Limits limit.

The creative mind abhors constraint by
any force. Ideas demand freedom to roam.

Some are cursed to live lives of misery as
prisoners in the wrong hemisphere of mind.

Passion is a fire which, when raging beyond
control, consumes cold reasoning with ease.

Frustration is an irrational response to reality.
We could think our way done with it.

Frustration is grounded in unwarranted
assumption that life should be much easier.

Frustration is contrary to a mind at peace
and a reason-based, much happier life.

Ancient hills withstand still the travails of
time. Like Love. Like Faith. And other rocks.

Memories bring joy again when long-past
happy times wash across our idle minds.

It is one of life's ironies that no love is free;
the greater the love, the greater its cost.

It's not Money that is at the root of all evil
but an often overabundance of Love-of-Self.

The nobility of some makes us proud to be
of the same species. Others … otherwise!

It's a challenge to embrace them, but It is
an honor to be despised by dishonorables.

The will to live contains within it the will to
maximize well-being. Best strive to thrive.

Live Love: in those two words, the sum of human wisdom for a happy, meaningful life.

Contentment is the reward one receives for desiring no more than he can strive to have.

All joys of rational thought come at the cost of frustration at its paucity in most others.

If the way you think detracts from your own contentment, best to rethink how you think.

When you think about it, how you think is a choice. The wise optimize life for happiness.

Left to roam utterly free, all creatures gravitate toward their own comfort zone.

For all God's creatures freedom to roam free is their ideal life; Contentment, their goal.

There are few greater joys than the joy of Understanding. Seek deeper insights always.

Insight is nothing more than a mystical
flash of sudden understanding in disguise.

Bifurcated Me: there's a merely mortal me
with a far nobler but weaker me inside.

From Knowing, Insight; from Insight,
Wisdom; from Wisdom, Clarity and Joy.

Art is image, never reality, never Truth itself
nor, most often, a reliable path to Truth.

Almost everything important in our lives is
earned incrementally, bit-by-bit, over time.

Little of lasting value or significance happens
in an instant. Except death. Best be patient.

Frustration, anger, hurt, despair—all are
issues of Control ... or rather, lack of it.

We have power to control how we respond
to those circumstances that disturb us.

We can, by force of will alone, choose not to
react as we do. Practice serenity ... thus Joy.

Dread not the cold winds autumn portends.
For some, winter may not come at all.

Serenity is an unfamiliar joy denied the
impatient. Trouble is, it's never easy.

Outlook is not everything. But it shapes
everything. Good news: outlook is a choice.

If Happiness were certain, easy or cheap, it
would surely lose its worth. Like much else.

Happiness is cherished, in part, because it is
difficult, rare & costly. It's goal of all desires.

Happiness is grounded in good habits
of right conduct. Every habit is a choice.

Mankind has progressed from primitive
barbarism to modern barbarism. Some gain!

Fools all, we squander our brief lives in
fevered pursuit of pleasure at cost of joy.

It's a moment of dread each aged year when
one must shorten the Christmas-card list.

There is hubris behind every assumption
that any of one's thoughts has real merit.

One's written thought is more arrogant still.
Written, it assumes lasting merit. Like this.

If sufficiently wise, the burdened chieftain
can still find tranquility within his own soul.

Nothing so soothes the mind as a conscience
at ease. More often, the reverse is also true.

One magical secret to happiness is to learn
to pause a second to cherish life's small joys.

The older I get, the higher my threshold for
amusement; guess I've heard the good stuff.

Call it arrogance, as far too many do, but there can be no genius without confidence.

What of emotional wisdom, the innate impulse to do right? Mothers are full of it!

Our identity rests upon our perceptions of who we are ... and, equally, who we are not.

The Other—our antithesis—is vital to our very Selves, very much a key part of us.

At the core of Life itself lies the compulsion to not only survive but to fully flourish.

Love it or hate it, Self is the first possession. Self, by definition, means Not Other.

Identity, is vital to all sentient beings. It demands differentiation from all others.

All beings with Identity—individuals or groups—must be in opposition to others.

Conflict, alas, is at the core of human nature and, truth told, nature itself ... in its entirety.

Nothing is worthwhile until the question has been answered and weighed: At what cost?

If you must inventory the losses, then count, too, the gains. And add in the bads avoided.

It is another of life's great inequities that Nobility is inequitably distributed. Like all.

Modesty is pretense, mere Vanity disguised— while perceived superiority is obscured.

Our modesty unwarranted, we are all too aware of our position in life's hierarchies.

The range of human attributes, value and accomplishment is vast. Equality is a mirage.

Truth is, customs foreign to one's own are as uncomfortable as new shoes that pinch.

Happiness transcends mood of the moment and fleeting circumstance. Instead, it abides.

What we truly, fervently feel cannot for long be concealed by the non-devious among us.

Insight bows not to will. I seem a passive instrument of Insight's self-expression.

The creeping sense of failure we feel as we age may be inching atrophy of enthusiasm.

The antidote to any sense of failure is to find something you really care about to pursue.

He who would receive must give freely: Respect. Tolerance. Empathy. And Love.

The tougher the opponent, the sweeter the victory. The effort demanded adds value.

Creativity and Conformity never peacefully coexists in the artistic Self. One must win.

All living creatures crave maximum freedom
to pursue their own perfected well-being.

Excellence of art is a thing apart, entirely
separate from the character of its creator.

Though neither art nor music, there can be
beauty still in a tightly reasoned argument.

Fallacious argument clangs as ugly against
the mind's ear as a rowdy child's tin drum.

Psychology can prove to be self-fulfilling.
If you think you have a neurosis, you do.

Nothing stands between Impulse and
Compulsion but the strength of willpower.

No values, no standards. No beliefs, no
values. Such qualities are interdependent.

All that we own is apart from us. All that we
love is a part of us. Love surpasses all things.

Insight, always sudden, startles us to new understanding, leaving us never the same.

Truth, Beauty, Liberty and Love: gifts of God, designed into things-the-way-they-ever-are.

Justice, Equality, Peace and Happiness are the noble but elusive aspirations of Man.

"Creative license" is the special prerogative claimed by talented elites to lie through art.

Never forget that Art is Art and Truth, Truth. Neither constrains the other. Believe Truth.

Emotion enslaves; Reason liberates. Fear Emotion but love Reason with full emotion.

One joy of growing old is the diminishing expectation of others for you to be "cool."

In youth, one wants nothing so much as to fly with the flock, to blend in, indistinctly.

With maturity, life's instinct demands an
unambiguous identity all one's own—a Self.

Reason is not without feeling, as thought.
Rather, there's inspiring Beauty in Reason.

Reason tells us that it is Reason that sets
us apart from all else in nature that lives.

Reason's gift provides us the liberty to make
free choices in pursuit of our well-being.

It is Reason, combined with Love, that best
defines us as human. So, best love Reason!

A book does not exist if it is not read. Nor
does a thought of love, if it is not said.

We pursue Happiness for its own sake; all
else in pursuit of Happiness, the end desire.

Beauty's mystic power often stirs the Soul.
Reason's mystic power can stir the Intellect.

Art is often like ice—a primal force for
destruction, alas for both good and bad.

Judgment is easy for the unencumbered
mind. Right judgment demands more.

Man alone is responsive to the bountiful
Beauty commonplace amongst us. Enjoy!

Without morality, there is no virtue. Without
virtue, Man is the worst of all the beasts.

Those who are bathed in treasures too often
treasure nothing. Call this Surfeit Syndrome.

To deprive your children of their potential
for failure would be cruel child abuse. Don't.

Paternalism should nurture and liberate,
never enslave and limit through over-love.

Why imprison yourself with anxiety over
what others think? Judge Self on substance.

It is not what others think that confines you but what you think they think that does it.

———◦◦◦———

The beauty inside does not erode as you age; it grows in proportion to your wiser virtues.

———◦◦◦———

Reason counsels us to put our minds to higher use than fruitless self-torture: angst.

———◦◦◦———

Happiness is never hostage to circumstance. It is a function of attitude. At end, a choice.

———◦◦◦———

Attitude is no captive of circumstance. It is a function, too, of choice, a controllable asset.

———◦◦◦———

Joyful is the mind self-taught to not think about what it chooses not to think about.

———◦◦◦———

Happiness is not the proper role of free government; freedom is, safety is, justice is.

———◦◦◦———

History is not destiny … at least for those who learn the right lessons from it. Study.

Worry is the popular unproductive act of preliving problems that may never happen.

Happiness is a just reward for right choices. Our potential for happiness is God's gift.

There is no place for haste in the enjoyment of fine wine ... or provocative philosophy.

Together, we are one, separate but, at base, inseparable, like fingers on a hand. Family.

One's lust for change atrophies with age as the craving for predictability grows stronger.

I'm alone in my mind, you see—nobody to see the true me I be. Save me. And God.

Most problems, it seems, can be traced to flawed and often unrecognized assumption.

The most troublesome assumption is that things will happen as we think they should.

Talent is uncommon skill driven by equally rare, undeniable compulsions to apply it.

To know the good son well is enough to know the mother's gift of Family was great.

In my own eyes, I am not absorbed so much with myself as within myself. Do you see?

Those ever in contention are never content. Serenity inevitably eludes contrarians.

It matters not that centuries may separate us. What unites us is Family. That's tiimeless.

All mortals err, in some degree, about everything. Except this assertion, you see?

We see the world not as it is but in absurd caricature. Webster: "grotesque imitation."

Judgment is best when it is suspended until understanding takes root. Only then decide.

To avoid burdensome thought, we distill the complicated into oversimplified certainties.

Drop a rock, it falls. That's a "miracle," like all universal truths. No particle is unruled.

Beware of those who read just a little. They tend to assume they know. Error looms.

Beware of those who think they know. They are easily recognizable by their certainty.

Unnecessary fear assaults Peace-of-Mind unnecessarily. Modern media thrive on it.

There are many ways to tell a story, but there is no way to tell the whole story.

The Self is the sum total of a person, both conscious and subconscious, ever evolving.

Identity is that portion of Self which is recognized by one's Self, and to others.

Culture is a vital force in our lives. Culture is our Collective Self, core of shared Identity.

If, in truth, I am wrong, let it be. It is far better for Truth to prevail than merely me.

Man's Rationality itself is grounded in the assumption of a pervasive rational universe.

Science's base assumption of a rational universe is grounded in a rational creation.

We all reduce Truth, ever complex, into inaccurate, variable oversimplifications.

The past is not only another time, it's another place. Alas! No visitors allowed.

Every tick of time brings into being a new reality, a unique sum of all that has been.

When Time ticks again, a whole new Reality begins, a new synthesis of all that is past.

A static state grows more appealing with age in the lengthening shadow of its end.

The consensus on consensus: the wider the weaker. Ever at odds, unanimity eludes us.

Distance obscures detail ... and clarity. Be wary of judging far things dimly perceived.

An idea can be both obvious and profound, often so obvious its profundity is obscured.

Truth, by its nature, denies the validity of alternatives. No contradictions allowed.

Beyond Knowledge, there is a Knowing that is more profound: knowing how to Know.

Tradition is not the past but rather its distilled essence, the best of past knowing.

It is criminal folly to cast Tradition aside without weighing the cost of what's lost.

Tendencies to cast aside worthy things because they're old is appalling. (I'm 90!)

Reality expands exponentially with each tick of Time, embracing again all that has been.

When early Man sought to understand the needs of survival, Reason's seed sprouted.

What you read here is a mosaic of insights with common grout: the pursuit of Truth.

From these random musings emerges, to my surprise, a coherent world view unsought.

What is IS. Reality is unaffected by the way it is perceived by us squabbling mortals.

Truth is Truth just as gold is gold. Where it is found matters not a jot. Its value is intrinsic.

To seekers of Truth within the complexity of all things, firm conclusions are ever denied.

To truth-seekers, every opinion is a rickety hypothesis ever vulnerable to new insight.

It is the mind's duty to make sense of the chaos to form a plausible neural narrative.

The mind's most important work is beyond the reach of consciousness. Alas, a mystery!

Long after knowledge is forgotten, the understanding from it remains. Keep at it.

Truth and Gold are much alike. Both are pure, rare, beautiful, elusive and enduring.

Truth and Gold differ, too. Gold is always treasured, diligently sought, never feared!

I'm not smart enough to judge how much smarter others, smarter, are than I am.

All genius is undervalued by the self-serving gap shrinkage of others. Ego demands it.

Like gravity, the ubiquitous Bell Curve of all attributes is a pervasive force among us.

———

To maximize Truth and Liberty, help strengthen those values as ideals for all.

———

Among Superman's amazing powers, none surpasses x-ray vision. Wisdom is akin.

———

Order demands it: nothing in nature is without cause, purpose, and consequence.

———

Without order, chaos rules. But all order requires force with purpose. God provides.

———

We are both blessed & cursed to live in our own times, like all those past and future.

———

The next generation of children is society's key link with all of humanity's tomorrows.

———

When he thinks, he who truly thinks, lives his hours of deep thought all alone, within.

It is not so much that Knowledge is required for Wisdom, but rather, reverse is the case.

It is not enough to Think. One must Think well. To Think well, one must Know. Learn.

The peace-of-mind so essential to happiness of all remains under unrelenting assault.

Pinpoints of ancient light, brilliant still, reveal evidence of Truth at a distant time.

Ideas gravitate toward absurdity just as order, sans control, gravitates toward chaos.

All living things are designed to strive to thrive. Tragically, those that don't, won't.

Each dwells at the bottom of his own well to stare up with unique vision of the same sky.

One can look at scriptures of ancient beliefs as treasure maps to the wisdom of the ages.

Unmined gold, like understanding, is there for those who search and determinedly dig.

There is nothing now so free, so accessible and so valuable as Knowledge ... but air.

With each retelling, and each new hearing, every story tends to drift farther from truth.

Deep wisdom rests on one's powers to grasp implications of disparate knowledge.

Wisdom demands a keen sense of the scale that separates amateurs from professionals.

Seek ever broadening perspective over All-That-Is. The view is well worth the climb.

I love Truth. More, I delight in it! Not just Truth but Truth honed to a sharp edge.

Mortals dissolve to grave dust, but the legacies of Aristotle and Mozart live on.

Transient tangibles seem far less real than the perpetual abstract forces that order all.

Every life has consequences where its more lasting values lie. Our effects roll on and on.

Great Truths can be derived by resolving smaller, more accessible component Truths.

Knowledge is value you acquire. Wisdom is a treasure you create. (Assembly required.)

Truth is complex. Conclusions about it are inherently (and necessarily) oversimplified.

Perceptive people, with varying perspectives and purposes, often differ on most things.

The intellectually honest Truth-seeker will not "cherry pick" but seek out Net Truth.

Fanned to fury by howling winds of mass media, Fear Fads rage like forest fires. Alas!

Ideas inherited from the accumulated past form the foundation of any civilization.

Receptivity to the potential for breaks with the past is essential for a better future.

Truth is difficult, elusive, complex, obscure —but bountiful. Our world is full of it. Seek it.

Reality clouds our lives often less than the stories of those who mislead about History.

The mind rises as it grows to higher vantage points and broader visions. Keep climbing.

To gain access to the tall timber of higher truths, first clear the thorny underbrush.

These Pearls are mere fragments, fleeting, elusive insights, frozen in time with words.

The mind makes its crucial step toward wisdom when it first turns inward on itself.

Any thought—even a fallacious thought—has value in its potential to provoke others.

Whatever one believes he knows is the source of whatever Truth he ultimately finds.

What we absorb makes us what we are. We become what we consume. EX: Knowledge.

Let Reality defend Rationality. Ultimately, Reality will prevail over Absurdity (we hope).

Most lack ability to recognize the relevance of concrete particulars to abstract principle.

Recognition of similarity among dissimilar things is evidence of far too rare wisdom.

What is Insight but a miraculous revelation previously unimagined? Such eludes will.

The past is all we know about the future. Predictions are too often predictably wrong.

There are legions of pragmatic materialists who have little patience with "abstractions."

Yet Truth itself is an abstraction—like Love, Beauty, Goodness, Liberty, Peace & Justice.

Thoughts of value wisely spoken are far too often foolishly heard. Many, deliberately so.

Skepticism is by far a more rational response than fear. But, tragically, fools choose fear.

Perfect knowledge is denied to all. There's 100% probability that no one is 100% right.

There is a story behind every story you hear, and another story behind that. Etc. Etc. Etc.

We stumble about in darkness, under the illusion that we see. Truth seen, is a glimpse.

My better insights rise up, unbidden. My subconscious is more perceptive than I am.

Forgetting is often treacherous—but almost always less so than remembering wrongly.

It is better than not to know when you don't know. To think you know when not is worse.

Youth's compulsion for action swamps the serenity necessary for wise reflection.

Those who truly love Truth, necessarily cherish Clarity and Authenticity as well.

Truth-seekers abhor: confusion, incongruity, ambiguity, muddle-mindedness, deception.

As best you can, catch and hold the durable truths that come your way. Make 'em yours.

It is through a natural, instinctive Truth-vetting that we accept Truth that fits us.

Truth extends to infinity with only a smidgen within reach of mortals. Most eludes us all.

The aging fertile mind turns irresistibly to introspection, searching for durable Truth.

———✦———

Thoughts tightly written are never crafted to be loosely read. Pay closer attention.

———✦———

A successful Pearl is a pithy wisdom that captures from insight a timeless principle.

———✦———

Truth and Wisdom are rare, and, being rare, alas, are too rarely recognized and prized.

———✦———

Man's greatest folly is to build conclusions upon conclusions of others, ignoring facts.

———✦———

Befuddled legions forever questions "Why?" But "Why?" implies reason, as if fools use it.

———✦———

A youth in mid-20s is years closer to the naiveté of childhood than adult wisdom.

———✦———

Experience be damned! All past is dead! The antsy idealism of youth fills in all the blanks.

To be ignorant is akin to being dead. Living, in essence, is knowing. Learn, and keep at it.

In obsession with trivia, visions of Truth float past us unseen like ephemeral cloud images.

Most Truth mystically morphs away in the turbulence, unacknowledged by lazy minds.

The leisure of retirement is an invitation to introspection, discovery of one's inner Self.

It is not only facts that divide us but our interpretations as shaped by world view.

One widely accepted world view denies Truth as true, a non-Truth about true Truth.

Without Truth as a standard, all is permitted … then chaos reigns supreme at great cost.

Only Truth separates us from destructive chaos and the inane idiocy of philosophers.

Faith vs Doubt: each is the antithesis of the other and thus gives meaning to the other.

To seek Truth requires that one have Faith that Truth exists and is worthy of pursuit.

Doubt shields against the error of mistaking what merely appears to be true to be Truth.

Be careful what you reject. Often even an atrocious idea may contain a seed of merit.

Between Black and White lie infinite shades and hues. Yet we mostly think in absolutes.

Our mortal minds exhibits an unlimited capacity for oversimplification. It's innate.

The insularity of the fool's mindset is akin to incest and, like incest, the outcome is idiocy.

In scoundrels or saints, nobles or knaves, genius is genius. Moral worth matters not.

Truth-seekers prize objectivity, yet, to
radicals, it is a shield for the status quo.

Each newborn comes equipped with an
equal (and infinite) supply of ignorance.

It's not art, but there is beauty still in a
tightly reasoned, fact-supported argument.

Fallacious, fluffy argument clangs ugly
against the mind's ear like a kid's tin drum.

Wrong ideas spring up, spread and smother
like kudzu to choke out minds of multitudes.

Wrong ideas multiply like weeds in rocky soil
where sprouts of real worth seldom survive.

Like a knife, Reason has great utility—for
good or evil or all shades in between.

Morality, like a knife, depends upon the hand
that wields it, not the instrument used.

Insights flutter about in twilight shadows of our thoughts like eager moths seeking light.

Truth is messy, a hodgepodge amalgam of contradictions and apparent irrelevancies.

Any story alleged to be true is the opposite. Simplification distorts Truth. Thus Story Bias.

The universal, overriding bias of any storyteller is the ever-edited story itself.

In short, any story is inevitably something other than Truth. Every story is a sales pitch.

All nonfiction is, in truth, fiction. What defines fiction is it's admission to untruth.

To foresee distant consequences is the essence of Wisdom, mostly denied youth.

All that I think, all that I believe, all that I am is rooted in all that I have learned and been.

All of humanity can imagine no more than a fragment of Truth, a smidgen of all that is.

Like fish in a pond, we swim in a tiny pool of our own circumstance we imagine is reality.

Every conclusion is a generalization—a synthesis of vast, conflicting complexities.

All abstract generalizations, necessarily oversimplifications, are other than reality.

Multitudes sleepwalk through a king's garden blind to insight's delights blooming.

Most amble aimlessly about, oblivious to all the beauty, absorbed in trivia, grumbling.

As I am, so I think. As I think, so I am. It is a closed-loop system. The Self is ever evolving.

We can never Know. By that, I mean, we can never know completely. Not anything. Ever.

It seems that we can know only partially. We can approach Truth, but never know it fully.

In aphorisms of great thinkers lies the treasure of eloquent and tested wisdom.

We are all prisoners of the thoughts of others. Strive to embrace the best of them.

There is no higher calling for the intellect than the pursuit of Truth. And that's true.

All other living things have this advantage over Man: they're incapable of irrationality.

Everything non-humans do is done with Reason. But, clearly, it is not their Reason.

After college, I have been largely self-taught with no curriculum to guide me but Interest.

What I have learned is random and spotty with vast emptiness in between, like islands.

Everyone has his own islands, dispersed
differently in the same Sea of The Unknown.

Burdensome leisure drives most to seek any
other than Thought to occupy empty hours.

The apathetic find ways to sleepwalk
through life, comatose to rich fascination.

Life is only as interesting as one's thoughts.
Non-thinkers are, in a sense, already dead.

The secret to wisdom is to carefully select
the things we choose to be ignorant about.

What has been shapes what will be. So it is
with our thoughts. None is without effect.

As best you can, get to the root of all things.
For clarity, understand origins and basics.

Interest is the compass of Thought. Without
interest, we are lost wilderness-wanderers.

Common Sense is practical wisdom. It knows no party, seeking best choices: to Optimize.

Many things we assume to be chance may well have their origins in human nature.

What we attribute to chance is statistically distributed natural propensities, it seems.

In this world, nothing is as certain as uncertainty. Of that, I'm certain. (I think.)

Any philosophical argument can and will be extended into absurdity by zealots zealously.

The art of philosophy is generalization. All generalizations are, to some extent, false.

A philosopher distills intoxicating essence from complex reality. No license required.

Selective knowledge is the only knowledge one can possess; selective truth, the same.

Abdicate thought-escape as a way of life. Thoughtlessness is not life but rather Death.

Thought cannot function without flawed assumption. And that's always the glitch!

Unacknowledged assumptions are the source of arguments about other things.

Einstein's single goal was to discover what he called "theories of principle." Same here.

Each mind is the unique sum of its own biology and experience. No two are alike.

When zealots are consumed by passions and rage, be sure reason has been abandoned.

It is unreasonable to reason with emotional people or to give credence to their cries.

I write what I think. What you think I think may be more what you think than I think.

Philosophers are few among the young. Like fine wine and friendships, they must age.

Consequences flow outward in concentric circles like ripples from a pebble in a pond.

Yogi was wrong. It ain't over even when it is over. All that was still is part of what will be.

All philosophy, and thought, for that matter, begins with doubt. Start there & think more

---

In order to think new thought one must first find doubt in what was previously thought.

One thought begets another just as one step suggests the next. And so, on and on it goes.

The stew that is you is unique. It is ever-changing, blending a flavor all your own.

We perceive effects; we infer causes–all too often inaccurately, frequently at our peril.

The effect of experience on each Self is much like a colorful kaleidoscope in constant flux.

———⋄⋄⋄———

All ideas are born in the context of existing ideas opposed, often inherently reactionary.

———⋄⋄⋄———

The catalyst for every idea is its opposition. To understand it, know what ideas it refutes.

———⋄⋄⋄———

Evil ideas must be opposed. They cannot be allowed to prosper and propagate. Resist!

———⋄⋄⋄———

More evil has resulted from evil ideas than all the greed and power lust of humanity.

———⋄⋄⋄———

The ability to derive general truths from disparate experience is talent, not learned.

———⋄⋄⋄———

General Truth, itself, is God's gift as is the uniquely human rare talent to perceive it.

———⋄⋄⋄———

The task of the mind is to structure ordered thought by selection and linkage of ideas.

The coin of this new age is Knowledge. The choice for all is clear: Learn or Languish.

To believe what one cannot know requires reason, faith, desire and a lot of hubris.

One can no more extract a storyteller from his story than personality from his person.

Every story is biased in its telling, every perception is biased by its perceiver.

Maturing is a process of peeling back the onion of understanding, one layer at a time.

Ignorance is an endless sea isolating tiny scattered islands of human understanding.

There's nothing so obvious as self-evident truth—once articulated by trusted others.

Most problems, it seems, can be traced to a flawed assumption. Beware of certainties.

The most troublesome assumption is that things will happen as they should. Wrong!

There is an intuitive "Knowing" which can transcend Knowledge. It is by far greater.

In the endless search for deeper Truth, each conclusion, in turn, becomes a new premise.

Each of us is unique ... and growing more so with every fleeting thought. No two alike.

If we believe things we cannot know, know, too, that we know things we do not believe.

Denied certainty, examine the evidence as best able, a dutiful juror, not expert witness.

Why is wisdom denied the young? Because Wisdom is experience-based, cumulative.

Age and experience are never enough or Wisdom would not be so rare and valuable.

There's an intellect involved in recognizing
useful Wisdom when it brushes against us.

Determined will is required in drawing
Wisdom in and making it a part of you.

Wisdom is sipped slowly and savored like
wine or breathed in like air and absorbed.

Wisdom is not knowledge. Nor is it intellect.
It is rare capacity for insight into high Truth.

To find Truth, or to even get close, one must
begin with a blank slate of suspended belief.

Some things seem destined to tangle, like
fishhooks, coat hangers, siblings and ideas.

The Wise hunger for wisdom; the unwise
have little appetite for it. It's a rare talent.

The complexity of our times forces a focus
on the narrow, or the shallow. Often both!

What is lost by busyness is capacity for deep thought and comprehensive understanding.

The mind is simple; yet the world, complex. Thus we all must generalize & oversimplify.

It inflates our egos to equate our imagined worth with the imagined most worthy.

In a world of designed-in infinite diversity there are unavoidable gaps in "Equality."

We are Equal only in our unrealized dreams of equal rights before law and God's eyes.

Axiom: Every problem's solution lies within its cause, a simple truth, usually ignored.

Strive to use "know" with precision, not as a synonym for "think" or "assume" like most.

To "know" has specific meaning with regard to Truth. Use words with precision. Know.

The great bulk of reported "News" is not
truth, but selected truth, mostly negative.

Think hard about how accurately "news"
reflects what we know to be genuine Truth.

Each of us is shaped to the precise contours
of his own biology and past, like jelly in a jar.

Our differences most often lie in opposing
attitudes, assumptions & resulting priorities.

You build those linkages that are uniquely
You in all of history, one synapse at a time.

One's chances of being both young and wise
are as remote as being both old and hip.

Some potential for wisdom may be revealed
in youth by a latent receptivity to wisdom.

Though some learn, priceless lessons pass
the young by as a breeze left by a flying bird.

The most important thing to know—and the most difficult of all—is that we don't know.

Know what you know. Know what you don't know. And know the important difference.

Effects from every cause affect effects from all other causes, like rain ripples on a pond.

All is connected. Understanding how is the pursuit of philosophy, science and religion.

In order to grow, one must relentlessly push outward the radius of his understanding.

Human understanding has limits, but limits never have been found, or even approached.

What we understand is that our limited understanding can always be expanded.

It is not sufficient to acquire knowledge; one must also think. Understanding is the goal.

Generalists, alas, are a vanishing species. In that sense, "progress" is self-defeating.

Knowledge, in our age, is cheap and easy to find. But Wisdom to use it is as rare as ever.

Time » Complexity » Specialization » Fragmentation » Conflict of Interests.

Among all societies, even the most primitive, there are wise, rare and unwise, plentiful.

Wisdom does not rest upon Knowledge, but the Wise compulsively seek it, knowingly.

Knowledge does not lead one to Wisdom, but rather Wisdom leads one to Knowledge.

History, alas, knows no shortage of foolish scholars but is rich with the wise otherwise.

The roots of hatred and prejudice can be deep, but so are the impulses to do right.

All mortals err, in some degree, about everything. Yet, the wise learn from error.

The object of Education is Knowledge.
The object of Knowledge is Understanding.

The object of Understanding is Wisdom. The object of Wisdom is mostly Right Choices.

The object of Right Choices is personal Happiness and The Greater Good.

The only "statement" I choose to make through appearance is "No comment."

Easy to say, harder to do, for me, maybe you, is that fools need empathy, too.

Culture, in the final analysis, is collective habit—and habit makes puppets of us all.

We have only to Love enough. Then, Peace and Hope and Justice and Joy will prevail.

Like Pearls, Insights most valuable are found at greatest depths. You have to dive deep.

Empathy is an invaluable talent, broadly distributed but in widely varying degrees.

In the young, denied Wisdom, it is sufficient that they be receptive to Wisdom and think.

Covet Wisdom even if you are not yet ready to achieve it. It grows from such tiny seeds.

Each of us is a far deeper pond than our surface reveals—especially to ourselves.

Explore your own depths. Treasures lie there that will otherwise slip quietly away, lost.

How much priceless ancient wisdom slipped back into the oblivion of our silent past?

The price of Free Will is Consequence. The reward for Free Will is Self. Self is first goal.

Err, if you must. But be wrong in the right direction for right reason at the right time.

Not-to-choose is not a choice. We all must choose and live with the consequences.

Notice and Fame are vastly overvalued by most who waste much of life on trivialities.

Pay no attention to me, stranger. I do not seek critique from those unimportant to me.

It's not attention or scrutiny from strangers that I crave. Rather, it is noninvolvement.

The less I am constrained by the irrelevant opinions of others, the greater my freedom.

Except for the people I care about truly caring about me, non-notice is my goal.

In the regard of others, if any, it is only substance, not style, that counts with me.

In existence, made up of infinite linkages of cause and consequence, everything matters.

Everything does not matter equally. Life's challenge is to discern what matters most.

"Common Sense" is a life-habit of thinking things through, minimizing acts of impulse.

Understand, Think, Do, in that order. Then, you'll be known for your "common sense."

A late bloomer, I took far too many years to figure out how much better I could be.

What is "cool" but elitism? What is elitism but pretense? What is pretense but a lie?

"Cool" is pretense to diminish and exclude others while falsely elevating Self. Uncool!

Every child, raised right, makes the world a better place, changing the density of Good.

It takes lots of ore to produce a little gold, a ton of knowledge for a little understanding.

Long after facts are forgotten, a treasure of understanding remains. So keep studying.

The more one understands, sadly, the more isolated he becomes from those who don't.

The praise of the fools is to be disdained. The disdain of the fools is to be prized.

God's gifts come to us in the form of our Potential. The rest is up to us. Duty calls!

Category judgments are inevitably in error and most often unjust applied to particulars.

Clearly, we cannot all become wise. But we can become wiser by yearning for wisdom.

To grow wiser, develop a lifetime habit of rubbing your mind up against true wisdom.

Not everyone can be wise. But anyone can be wiser with sufficient interest and effort.

When a good idea breaks a good principle, forego the idea, not ever the good principle.

To understand any idea, philosophy or principle trace its lineage back to its origin.

A feigned haughty attitude is often deemed necessary in absence of genuine substance.

An echo is nothing, a fleeting, empty sound, devoid of substance. Trust your own voice.

The ideal ideal is too often simultaneously inspirational and unattainable. So, stretch.

Like a rose, Love grows or it goes. Tend your garden with care. Use empathy as nutrient.

When people earn what they get and get what they earn, Justice is done. More hurts.

Happiness, boiled to essentials, is Love plus Peace-of-Mind. Alas, Love is the easy part.

Every path leads somewhere. Be sure that's where you want to go before stepping on it.

To truly Perceive is a wonder. To Know is pure joy. To Understand is utterly sublime.

Any culture's moral worth can be calibrated by how it values its children and its women.

It is not enough to Think. One must Think well. To Think well, one must truly Know.

Each wrong choice exacts its price. Each right choice brings its own reward. Justice.

Most endure tragically cramped little lives buffeted about by whim and circumstance.

Gourmet meals should not be gulped. They should be savored, bite by bite, like books.

By the free choice of bad habits we forge our own chains. Better habits is the key.

The foundation addiction upon which all other addictions rest is self-indulgence.

Like an aged tree, life's potentials branch out in divergent directions-never-taken.

Live such a life that you can stand in the lengthening shadows of old age, content.

The relationship between Effort and Value is direct. Value is rarely gained without effort.

Contrary to advertising, Happiness is more dependent upon Contentment than Elation.

Contentment eludes the impatient young who, in any event, show little taste for it.

Wrong ideas wreck lives ... and alter the destiny of civilizations. History has spoken.

Happiness is habit—Good Habit. It can be cultivated and strengthened with practice.

There are few higher honors than to be despised by the dishonorable among us.

Happiness, the end object of all desire, has deadly rivals named Anxiety and Ennui.

If we only do what is right to avoid due punishment or gain rewards, we do wrong.

We should do what's right because it's right in the interest, at end, of the Greatest Good.

There are ample facts all about to support conclusions of almost anyone's opinions.

Today's conclusions become tomorrow's premises, and so it goes, on into infinity.

Take care what train you board 'lest you find its destination not where you want to go.

There's no way to return to where you are.
On life's train, expect no round-trip tickets.

In this society, the wall between poverty and economic well-being is usually Ignorance.

In this technological age, the wall between knowing and not knowing for most is Will.

All that thwarts Will is Attitude which can be adjusted from within by conscious choice.

The essentials for a strong, lasting, loving relationship are Faith, Trust and Reciprocity.

It is wise practice to experiment with nothing you'd not welcome as an irresistible habit.

Much of what is desirable about that to be changed may be changed in the process.

To be or not to be is not the question, Bard. The question is: what to be ... and how?

If each of us would only be what we ought to be, imagine what a good world this would be.

———⚬⚬⚬———

Thus, to be what we ought to be is the most worthy of life's goals. Without will we won't.

———⚬⚬⚬———

There is always a best choice among our alternatives. We ought to choose that one.

———⚬⚬⚬———

All that we are imposes limits by defining all that we are not. Choose what not to be.

———⚬⚬⚬———

All that is Good passes judgment upon all that is not. There's no avoiding choice.

———⚬⚬⚬———

There can be no justice in judgment of our antecedents who lived in a different ethos.

———⚬⚬⚬———

Any living thing is simultaneously what it is and what it will be. Life includes potentials.

———⚬⚬⚬———

The worth of anything (life, too) combines both its present and its full potential value.

Without the intervention of Reason, all behavior gravitates toward the absurd!

All living things have the right—and the duty to all—to pursue their own well-being.

Good writers stand ready to edit first drafts; good thinkers, to edit their first thoughts.

A sure path to error is to latch on to and follow through first impulse. Edit thyself.

What is True? What is Right? What is Best? These answered, our course becomes clear.

The way others interact with us is influenced by the way we interact with them. Be gentle.

We are, in effect, locked together in a dance to the end. In all truth, no one acts alone.

It is egocentric foolishness to blame others without accepting our share of outcomes.

Our concerns broaden as options narrow, pyramid-like, with age. Options expire, too.

The ways in which the world interacts with me are unique. Change, if any, is up to me.

The martyr parent's sacrifice imposes imprisoning guilt on the child. Use care.

The good and wise parent's duty is to give the child's life to the child! Not his own.

Self-realization is essential to whatever well-being we impart to others. Be good to Self.

Ego is the necessary sacrifice to anyone's harmonious relationships. But protect Self.

Rage and clarity cannot co-inhabit the same mind. Clarity demands emotional restraint.

A personal Never-Do List is a helpful map to The Right Path. Begin with "I do not lie!"

One has only to deny the Lie to help assure a virtuous life. It is a Lie that shields every sin.

Healthy doses of uncertainty and skepticism are essential components of a reasoning life.

When it comes to relations with friends and family, make molehills out of mountains.

When facing choice between conflicting goods, choose always the greater good.

To enjoy Joy, practice determined Serenity by controlling Expectation and Reaction.

Toast, well-done: May we all live long, stay healthy, treasure happiness, and end easy.

Yearn far less for the regard of strangers. Rather, strive to do always what is right.

Do right, you will earn regard from all who cherish right, then disregard wrongdoers.

I can't fix the world. But I can do my part by fixing me. All I need do is do what I should.

Each of us is a unified whole. Every facet is interactively part of who and what we are.

We are what we are in total. With free will to be otherwise, we only are responsible.

We are responsible for ourselves. Not our parents, not society, not circumstance—us.

I'd take great pride in being among the last to surrender any ideal I cherish as worthy.

When my last ethos Alamo falls, my legacy would be honored to be its last defender.

The clearly Bad demands improvement, but Adequacy is a universally acceptable result.

Sad to say, but nothing achieves Excellence without exceeding Adequacy at added cost.

Excellence is inevitably the rare exception. The Ubiquitous Bell Curve always prevails.

Morality's only weapon in the war for values is the spear of Conscience, sadly blunted.

At 88, the absolute best advice I can devise, distilled to essence, is to Optimize all things.

The simplicity of "Ideal Choice" obscures its universal profundity as the best outcomes.

"Ideal Choice" blends with the wisdom of Aristotle's "Golden Mean." Perfect tradeoff.

We are the main authors of our children's memories. Childhood memories? Up to us.

It's not the big one-time events but the treasured traditions children cherish for life.

By far, the hardest part of professionalism is consistently making what they do look easy.

Consider your solemn responsibility to those
closest to you to be happy within yourself.

In my own distilled vision, the wise Buddha's
"Eightfold Path" boils down to Right Habits.

Good thought? Best to write it down, lest
it be lost in the dark labyrinth of the mind.

All that makes you You is Habit: Personality.
Preferences. Biases. Impulses. Opinions. All.

Everything that makes you unique relies on
Habit. And habits are a malleable choice.

Respect and nurture your natural gifts. They
are your blessing ... and your responsibility.

Look back two generations to understand
that we are no longer who we were then.

Look ahead 50 years and you'll understand
who we are now too soon will no longer be.

Much of what we cherish now as good is destined to dissolve in the mist of memory.

For each of us who becomes more noble in his own heart, humanity is enriched in kind.

Let the better world you yearn for begin first in your own heart, then work outward.

With each transgression, a fragment of character is lost. Age too often corrupts.

Every relationship is a dance. Every dance is unique. Step on as few toes as possible.

With Will, we can do or not do what we want. But we can't want what we want.

We must all, of necessity, be ignorant of some things. Be ignorant of the right things.

Be ignorant about the transient trivia of the present but never about the significant past.

It is in the substantive past where all the
great and hard-won lessons of humanity lie.

―⸺―

Ethics like Honor evolve irresistibly beyond
their ideal toward the extreme: Ethos Creep.

―⸺―

In the end, Time and Excess are the mortal
enemies of every Ethos. Thus, Ethos dies.

―⸺―

Those ever in need to occupy their minds
have understocked mental warehouses.

―⸺―

The bane of boredom tortures the sluggish
yet holds no threat to well-stocked mind.

―⸺―

The Principle of Principles: be guided by
principle over impulse and circumstance.

―⸺―

To recognize and avoid Wrong, one must
first have a clear, sharp vision of Right.

―⸺―

To know what is right is easy; to do what is
right, difficult. But right choice is ever right.

Legions are damned to miserable lives, dysfunctional as hapless habit puppets.

Left free to roam, like a rental horse with loose reins, we find our best way home.

To cut a diamond, use another diamond. To break a habit, use another habit. It's hard.

In default mode, most organisms compute short-term rewards. Only the Person plans.

When sandbass are spawning, fish hard. When thoughts are spawning, think hard.

May the urge to absorb new understanding sweep you forward breathlessly, my son.

Conformity is a tyrant who rules us all; few are truly free. Nonconformists are included.

Emotion is the rebel sibling of Thought, residing in the same mind but more willful.

If you think life is meaningless, it is. If you think life is meaningful, it is. Your choice.

Nonconformists cluster together, too, just another form of conformity. All of us do.

Everyone, if he chooses, has ample time to do what is important by doing less that isn't.

To be despised by the despicable is a true honor. Never allow enemies to define you.

Frauds and cheats make lousy victims. Those trustworthy make ideal patsies.

The better you write, the better you think. The better you think, the better you write.

Every thought, every act is a choice; every choice has a price. Duty is to choose wisely.

Human existence is observably designed so that any wrong choice has its ultimate price.

Each right choice has its ultimate reward.
Thus, Justice in the end eventually prevails.

———⚬⚬⚬———

To observe a universal effect and infer a universal cause is the essence of reason.

———⚬⚬⚬———

Cherish master blessings: Life. Love. Family. Happiness. Health. Truth. Liberty & Justice.

———⚬⚬⚬———

Acts often reveal much about their intent. From its fruit, much is learned of the tree.

———⚬⚬⚬———

Faith is reasonable when based on inference drawn from evidence of Existence & Order.

———⚬⚬⚬———

Transient truths are Man's domain; Durable Truth is God's alone. God deals in durables.

———⚬⚬⚬———

Every Durable Truth is part and parcel of a Higher Truth, all parts coherent, reinforcing.

———⚬⚬⚬———

"Believe!" commands every dogma as its first imperative. WHAT to believe is at issue.

For every opinion and ideology there's an
equally passionate opposite. No consensus.

Clearly, since we are all unique in apparently
every way, we are all meant to differ.

All living things have purpose essential to
their well-being and our common purpose.

The condition most essential for any pursuit
of purpose, is the freedom to do so. Be free.

Doubting and seeking are not indications of
faith deficiency. Truth is, quite the opposite.

One does not seek without faith that that
which is being sought is worthy & findable.

Seeking Truth validates faith that Truth
exists, is worthy and within reason's reach.

Human well-being, personal happiness and
moral good. The relationship of all is direct.

What Man has not created, he has found—discovered. What he's created is from that.

The potential within all that is—including Man himself—has an ultimate single source.

It would be more absurd than not to assume bountiful potential of all has no purpose.

No thing is a thing within itself, independent of cause & consequence. All that is is linked.

No thing is self-created in isolation from the rest. Every thing is part of the whole thing.

God is the author of all Durable Truth. If not, then who is? What then is its source?

With each new insight into Truth, one gains another glimpse of God. (i.e., Whole Truth.)

God's great gift of potential to do The Good surely carries with it the obligation to do so.

No one truly knows anyone—not even themselves. As any act of God, this is Good.

There is no mind on earth, nor has there ever been, like that of Einstein. Or, oddly, mine.

What we conclude about any thing rests heavily on what we have concluded before.

Timeless Pattern: Success › Hubris › Excess › Error › Consequences › often Ruin.

Somewhere, hard to find in between—lies old Aristotle's ever elusive "Golden Mean."

That form of government works best for all which gives maximum free rein to genius.

Love me for who I am, not for the things I think. Yet what I think makes me who I am.

Key keys to genius: hard work, persistence and an abiding reverence for excellence.

TV is a tyrant, forcing focus of our thoughts. Why surrender to a dumb box in the corner?

To choose is to judge. To judge is to have standards. To have standards discriminates.

With age perceptive senses seem to sharpen ... as if they know it will too soon be dark.

Distortion, obfuscation, delusion—tools of tyrants—are just more devious ways to lie.

Because diversity is universal, equality is nonexistent and hierarchy inevitable. Alas!

Self, simply, is the sum of one's habits. Culture is the sum of our shared habits.

With time to reflect, remnants of dormant knowledge coalesce to new understanding.

Without some sense of a core Truth as his connection with All, Man alone is lost, adrift.

One key to Happiness is Character. One key
to Character is Virtue. Virtue ebbs with age.

No one is so disdained by knaves and fools
as the inevitably rare incorruptible man.

A healthy Self is independent, free. A
parent's duty is to liberate his child's Self.

Politics = Power ever based on reciprocal
favoritism. Thus, it is by its nature, corrupt.

When it comes to Happiness, matter doesn't
matter. It is attitude and wisdom that count.

What matters are matters such as Love,
Family, Trust, Liberty, Truth, Peace, Justice.

Professionalism rests upon genuinely caring
how well the doing gets done, at any level.

The state-of-mind of the doer, not the task
at hand, makes the difference. Truly care.

Live on in the souls of your progeny to think rightly, live honorably and cherish Truth.

Nothing in the cosmos has Man's power of Reason and his sense of his own relevance.

It has been a long, hard road for those who came before us to arrive here. Judge gently.

Where we are is where we are. The net effect of history is the best we've had in us.

Cherish what we have achieved and do not hastily condemn those who came before us.

Though malcontents complain, history's sum is not the work of knaves, fools & evil kings.

The lesson in sailing, as in life, is to exult in every rare perfect, but transient, moment.

Who we are, what we think, and how we act confine us. Every thought, alas, is a shackle.

Workers are driven by others; strivers drive themselves. Attitude sparks achievement.

Law must be clear & precise to be obeyed but vague & ambiguous to be passed –alas!

Good mentors both inspire and restrain. Rule 1: Fan the spark, but restrain the flame.

Where there is choice, whatever it is that we earnestly seek we are most likely to find.

There's something special in the character of pioneers who ventures into the unknown.

The uniqueness of each mind is God's gift. Differences of opinion that result, another.

Much of the genius in geniuses lies in making the marvels they do seem effortless to others.

The years may pass, but they remain with us still. All that was lives on as part of what is.

The more we embellish our own fictions, the more we disbelieve any contradictory other.

All of us humans stare up at the same night sky and search for patterns we will to exist.

Give that matchless spark within you the air it needs to glow. Fan the flame for the light.

Summon the courage to rise above yearning to blend in with the herd to escape notice.

In the nonentity you crave lurks the sure loss of your uncertain and ever too-timid Self.

Embrace your uniqueness; share that which is special with others. Enrich their lives, too.

Man alone shares, however minimally, in the pervasive rationality ruling the universe.

Man stands alone, unique, in his ability to glimpse his own significance & insignificance.

Could it be merely hubris, or is it Truth, that the most wondrous creation of all is Man?

I was 73. It was harvest time--time to gather together scattered insights to distill Truth.

The challenge for fathers is for each to be a better father than his own father was to him

---

The only thing human that is all-inclusive is Humanity. For every Us, there is a Them.

Because of universal diversity there can be no unity. Like amoeba, we divide naturally.

Unrevealed Potential awaits opportunity to be shaped to beautiful proportions in time.

Light prevails; life goes on. Calm your mind. Lift your soul. Let your heart be content.

Weed & Flower, Bush & Tree—all live things share in the universal yearning to live free.

Two implied Commandments cry out to us:
"Thou shalt live." "Thou shalt live free."

The ceaseless assaults of Change prevail, but incrementally, and at high cost in casualties.

Along the way, too late, I lost my early ambition to be unobtrusively ordinary.

I feel at times blessed, at times cursed, with inexplicable vision to see obscure things.

On reflection, my greatest error, like most, was too low expectation for life's potentials.

It is the mind's duty to make sense of the world, work mostly beyond consciousness.

It's commonplace for people to share shards of their Selves with those closest to them.

Pioneers who broke away from the security of settled society were truly a breed apart.

Perplexed? Try imagining a world in which the irritant that plagues you did not exist.

Man alone is capable of marvelous responses to our bountiful Beauty.

Urgency, inevitably, is the enemy of Efficiency, Efficacy and Excellence.

Never a real philosopher, I might be more accurately described as an Insightcatcher.

The Self grows, slowly emerging from infancy, then evolving over a lifetime.

Unlike the atrophying cellular body, the Self grows ever stronger, deeper, fuller, uniquer.

The more one understands, the more isolated he becomes from those who don't.

Conquest is a motive force for civilization. Man's evils, too, serve the Ultimate Good.

The object is not to grow wiser; we all grow wiser with age. The task: Grow wiser faster.

———∞———

Principles are not inventions of Man but are rather discovered, much like laws of nature.

———∞———

Philosophy « » Reason « » Wisdom « » Truth « » Honesty « » Commonsense.

———∞———

Each new instant of Is compounds all that Was. Existence is exponentially cumulative.

———∞———

Success in marriage demands a reasoned reconciliation of many incompatible habits.

———∞———

A child is like a message in a bottle set afloat on the uncharted sea of the future. Careful!

———∞———

Deviation from routine trivia demands focus of mind vastly better used for deep thought.

———∞———

Cultivated Habit—like automatic pilot—is a useful tool for optimum mind management.

To truly love is to love fully. To love fully is to trust. To trust and love involve very real risk.

The cost of love is risk, the reward for love is Happiness ... if you can with peace-of-mind.

Beware the Master Sin: Excess. It not only magnifies all sins but corrupts every virtue.

Nothing is simple. Nothing is easy. Nothing stays fixed. Learn that; live frustration-free.

Government, with the power to make and enforce law, is restrained only by the law.

We all feel ennobled by the degree of villainy we perceived in our despised opponents.

History is clear: Liberty is an aberration. Tyranny, alas, is history's default condition.

Your mind has a powerful grip on your circumstance. So, never surrender to it.

We construct our lives through choice after choice at the cost of unexplored potentials.

To never entertain views challenging your own is to burn unread books in your mind.

Predictable things everywhere offer convincing evidence of God's miracles.

Infallible predictability is a phenomenon beyond the capabilities of mere mortals.

Beneath the infinite diversity of the universe there is a single unifying force: Truth is!

Expect reason from no bureaucracy. They are not ruled by Reason but by procedure.

All that is is the grand synthesis of all that has been. Past compounds into the future.

Inherent in knowledge of Good and Evil is the sense that humanity forever falls short.

Falling short is the price of any ideal, any standard, any worthy goal in human life.

———∞———

That we can never achieve our own ideals does not render the idea of ideals as wrong.

———∞———

"Have Faith!" we are implored. "But I need Proof!" multitudes retort, as if faith is folly.

———∞———

There are some things one ought to believe for his own happiness, provably true or not.

———∞———

The Empathy Impulse is that commonplace human propensity for intuitive sympathy.

———∞———

Charity and manners are learned, but the propensity for empathy, it seems, is innate.

———∞———

Empathy, tho variable, is essential to human survival, a primal attribute with great utility.

———∞———

Try to imagine existence without faith in the predictability of the laws of the universe.

Universal vastness lessens not the wonder in the creation of a grain of sand. Or Man.

The uniqueness and significance of Man is not diminished by whatever else there is.

The default destiny of Man is evil. Untaught, he will become a monster and soon perish.

Which is greater, the Idea of a thing or the thing itself? The Idea of the thing is durable.

Which is greater, some thing loved or Love itself? Some thing beautiful or Beauty itself?

For a richer life, mine the mountain of life's trivia for more meaningful moments. Dig.

One who never fails fails to risk enough. One who fails often risks too much too often.

Wisdom and Common Sense are exquisite cloth woven from the same precious thread.

In compound sentences joined by "but," what comes after the "but" is remembered.

"Risk, Originality and Virtuosity." (ROV formula to win of an Olympic champion.)

All truths are linked, as in a giant crossword puzzle, integral to the Grand Unity—Truth.

The Will ceases to be Free when it becomes the voluntary prisoner of Impulse. Be Free!

We mellow with age to reflect the growth of wisdom to appreciate joys of serenity.

Old age has its compensations for loss of youth. Wisdom outweighs exuberance.

Learn to cherish free uncertainty. There's crushing certainty in the life of a prisoner.

If you cannot find Contentment within yourself, who else can be content with you?

Generally, writers are contemplative, unobtrusive, solitary but, too often, lethal.

History, on balance, is clear: writers wreak more havoc than armies & are more feared.

Where is the virtue in Right without Wrong? In Good without Bad? Choice is a treasure.

What is a "rational" choice? Choice that advances the Greater Good. Others aren't.

When Whim and Will struggle for control of one's life, Happiness hangs in the balance.

Whim is the slave of Emotion; Will is the tool of Reason. Fight for Reason's victory.

Oh the comfort, the ever blissful comfort, of being with others who think like me!

What is a mind worth? What could it be worth with proper cultivation? Study.

Beware the danger of enslaving dependents through over-dependence. Help them grow.

The corruption of ideals begins at the very moment Truth is subordinated to ideology.

The price of Freedom is Democracy. The price of Democracy is restraint of Freedom.

Common Sense is practical wisdom. One discovers it in all levels of sophistication.

Bureaucracies abhor variance. Human beings are variable. Rules rule ruthlessly.

Dependence is another form of slavery; paternalism, another form of tyranny.

Economic Justice = Equal Opportunity + Unrestricted Potential Realization.

Peasants make scant history ... except in revolt. If victorious, others then rule change.

In journalism, the bad news is that there's seldom any good news—by definition.

———

Ideology enslaves the mind; zealotry enslaves the mind completely. Stay free.

———

Awe among the masses is key to power of tyrants. So, castles of old glowed with gold.

———

Trust and Truth are like fraternal twins— not identical but of the same substance.

———

Socialism is a system designed to optimize adequacy at the high expense of excellence.

———

Democracy has two allied mortal enemies. Their names are Ignorance and Apathy.

———

Durable change is always incremental. The more significant the change, the more so.

———

Art often acts as ice. It can be used as a primal force for change by revolutionaries.

Distilling core Truth to bite-size ideas like these may be the art of Maxim-izing.

What kind of world would this one be if everyone else thought like me? Boring!

All that thwarts Will is Attitude, and that can be adjusted from within & potentials bloom.

Why strive for a better life if any advantage gained thereby is negated at will by others.

If all runners are awarded equal prizes, it is predictably certain to be a slow & dull race.

Every new idea alters, however slightly, the complex collective ethos—the "Ethology."

Choose direction before walking. Think before talking. Understand before deciding.

Both the Foolish and the Wise are defined by their choices. Be wise and choose wisely.

Two kinds of fools: those who don't know
their choices are foolish and those who do.

———⊸◉⊶———

Anything has purpose, perhaps in potential
yet to be realized in the remote future.

———⊸◉⊶———

They are "pushers," too, whose rare talents
push narcotic ideas that poison our culture.

———⊸◉⊶———

All stories are biased, but some are less
objectionable in views judged congenial.

———⊸◉⊶———

All significant perspectives grow out of one's
world view. Any issue is not the issue itself.

———⊸◉⊶———

It's daunting and rare to change people's
mind on anything grounded in their outlook.

———⊸◉⊶———

It is logically impossible to do and be Good
without the freedom to choose otherwise.

———⊸◉⊶———

Rational, contemplative, law-abiding,
tolerant & forgiving folks are rotten in a riot.

A truly effective riot takes a lawless mob of emotionally driven wreckers, mad as hell.

I've learned to listen to my inner self, which seems to know far better than merely me.

Cold and controlling logic alone too often is prone to lead us astray. Emotion is worse.

Where there is diversity there must also be limits to allow for distinctions of identity.

Without identity, there can be no Self, no Them, or no Us. Without Us, there's no me.

As much as we try to mush all things together, boundaries are essential.

Education is knowledge we gain from others; Insight is knowledge we gain from our mind.

I am at odds with most, craving substance as escape from trivia rather than the reverse.

Beauty gravitates to the upper classes.
Beauty attracts wealth and vice versa.

Premises persist, even when the conclusions
they lead to have long since proven wrong.

All living things strive for short-term rewards
… except for the rare humans who succeed.

How did I arrive here? Not through "luck" or
chance but choices of my own at real costs.

Arguing politics is wasted wind. Best try to
distill your disagreements to first principles.

Power, like spilled raw blood, coagulates with
time into a solid, messy, sour mass.

We set out on the long, difficult journey to
Liberty and wound up in License instead.

Mansion or hovel, the mind is home. It
is furnished piece by piece with ideas.

Long after my trivial tasks are irrelevant, the value in the transient thoughts remain.

Much is unknown, yet clues, intuitions and evidence suggest vastly more to know.

Free Will, Choice, Good and its opposite, Evil, are necessarily tightly interwoven like cloth.

Light lurks in every darkness. Each moment of misery brings its inevitable end nearer.

The Soul: One can never know what it is. Or if it is. But always, Man has sensed that it is.

The Soul is something primal, everlasting, somehow akin to the very seed of one's Self.

The universality of Man's shared sense of Soul is convincing testimony that the Soul is.

The understanding in one mind can never be transferred with exactness to another mind.

Each understanding is unique, shaped by the unduplicated context of all that was before.

One mind can give another access to understanding, never understanding itself.

Understanding must be both sought and welcomed to be earned by its receiver.

The transmittal of understanding occurs only as a symbiosis, between sender to receiver.

All too often I stumble upon insights of ancients I thought I thought on my own.

Wonders are discovered spelunking in the mind. But avoid getting lost in the labyrinth.

Gleaning Truth is not just a hobby for me; it is a source of nourishment. And, I find it fun!

At any instant, I am all that I have ever been, all that I am, and all that I shall ever be. Me.

The purpose of Reason is the Good, not just individual Good but God's Greater Good.

I frolic here with my insights, like a child in a sand box of his own mind with toys ignored.

The most critical stage of any conscious act precedes the act itself. Aim first, then shoot.

Free choices have deserved consequences. Usually, we earn the fruits of our decisions.

Success in life boils down to the degree to which we have approached our potential.

Habitual rationality is akin to religion in a way, prodding us insistently toward right.

The grandeur of kings had political purpose: awe among the multitudes is key to power.

It is seductive emotionality, rarely cold rationality, that often leads us astray.

All are flawed. And no one of us knows enough about any other to judge degree.

Concessions will never placate ideologues. A placated ideologue ceases to be one.

People, like wildebeests, thunder this way, then that, controlled by blind herd anxiety.

We don't change how people think. If they change, they have to change themselves.

From "Tom Sawyer," we long ago learned that danger lurks in abandoned minds.

We are all shaped by the thoughts of others. But which others is our own free choice.

Nothing is without consequence. And every consequence has its own consequences.

Everything that is has Potential. Thus, true value of anything includes all of its Potential.

To make a humble cowman cringe at your ignorance, use your elbow to roll up a rope.

If you wish for others the joy and freedom of self-realization, teach them self-reliance.

Polarization is a self-perpetuating process. Each excess provokes an opposite excess.

The all-too-human urge to oppose is ingrained in our nature. Disagree?

Paternalism crushes self-realization, and thus Identity--even Self. It's akin to slavery.

Our aging Ethos is ebbing rapidly away, like beach surf sand beneath my sensitive soul.

Happiness, unlike transient exhilaration, does not depend on its acknowledgment.

True Happiness is more like the silent Gulf Stream than the tempest of a sea squall.

Happiness doesn't wash over us in rogue waves of elation but abides like peace.

Life is predictably discriminatory against those who decline to strive and smile.

If I could fix the world, I wouldn't. The world is more capable of fixing itself than I could.

Knowledge is finite; Ignorance, infinite. There's no real contest! Learn, Baby, learn.

What natural thing is not worth its creation? All that is has Purpose. Waste, then, is sinful.

Remember: each of us has a finite amount of attentiveness. It is best used prudently.

When Principle does not trump its inevitable challengers, it ceases to remain Principle.

When teachers pass into past, students look back with regret for not listening more.

Work gravitates to the competent and willing. The reward for good work is more.

To assess the worth of anything, imagine in vivid detail our Existence deprived of it.

The curse of the competent is that their rare value precludes their promotion to higher jobs.

I wish for others who wish for others: A long life, good health, happiness and an easy end.

Justice, too, is grounded in Empathy. Empathy is voluntary, never edicted.

To learn a new word is to expand one's range of consciousness with new meaning.

Ingredients for human well-being: Ambition, Ingenuity and Energy as essential values.

It would advance the cause of liberty to consider all force upon others as evil.

Force is evil though it may well be justifiable evil in those cases where it is necessary.

When imagined nobility is won by imposing force upon others, it may be tyranny instead

---

Feeling self-righteous? Beware! Much of the greatest evil was born of noble impulse.

The only defense against power is counterbalancing power. Newton's Law.

Linked meanings: Philosophy. Reason. Wisdom. Truth. Honesty. Commonsense.

The individual is the ultimate minority whose rights, above all, must be protected.

Nothing is simple. Nothing is easy. Nothing stays fixed. Learn that to combat frustration.

The individual is a one-celled organism, the irreducible entity of independent choice.

Human well-being depends upon the degree to which Truth, Reason and Liberty prevail.

An authoritarian regime depends upon regimentation of society's habits of thought.

Those ignorant of history live out their lives as amnesia victims in the perpetual present.

The net of History's progress is the sum of man's cumulative wisdom minus his errors.

To become more than you are, ask bigger questions & seek more substance, less trivia.

Life is like peeling a peach: the longer you keep at it, the more tenuous your grip on it.

I understand far more than I know, yet, I know far more than I understand, loop-like.

The goal of Learning is not so much to Know as it is to Be. Understanding » knowledge.

Education is knowledge we gain from others;
Insight is enlightenment we mine from mind.

I realize I am at odds with humanity, craving substance as I do as an escape from trivia.

Premises somehow persist, even when the conclusions they lead to prove to be wrong.

With diversity, there also must be self distinctions. Identity demands distinctions.

Without Them, there can be no Us. Without Us, there can be no I. Boundaries are a must.

Bureaucracies are compelled by their nature to limit Freedom. Thus, the fewer the better.

It seems evident that any creator loves his own masterwork as the very essence of Self.

Ideological blinders make fools of great intellects. History's examples are legion.

It is self-limiting to reject great art because of imperfections in the artist. Judge results.

Take care. Only a heartbeat separates us from the oblivion of all that used to be.

Be of good cheer. All the trivia that troubles you will soon be gone. "This, too, will pass."

Between Conflict and Tolerance lies Reasonable Persuasion. It's bloodless.

God is the pitch to which the music of the spheres is attuned. If we could only hear.

Skepticism and contrary arguments are needed shields for vulnerable truth-seekers.

Tell me the story and I'll tell you the bias of the storyteller. Every story is biased thereby.

The swifter the current, the closer the falls and all the more certain our too-late fate.

Success in marriage demands a difficult reconciliation of incompatible habits.

Look at any glorious sunset and witness the death of another day unique in all eternity.

Sunsets are splendid but sad—the passing of the old as a necessary sacrifice to the new.

The object is not to grow wiser. We all grow wiser. The object is to grow wiser faster.

That quiet but insistent voice within has proven over a lifetime to be my best advisor.

Procedures abhor exceptions; Rules rule … ruthlessly. Bureaucracy: a rule-based system

---

Political Polarities: The more radical one is, the more radical his opponents seem.

Whether I shake my rake at the ever-raining leaves now or tomorrow matters little.

Capturing a fleeting thought of long-term worth in the magic of the moment counts.

Perhaps, in time, when some stranger will engage these insights, I'll again see the light.

Fish who live their lives in polluted ponds never miss the fresh water. That died, lost.

My grandchildren and theirs will grow old never missing the good that was, then gone.

Reality's dichotomous. There's humanity's transient things and God's durable domain.

Approach with care the potential for latent tyranny in every well-meaning act of charity.

Values, like gifts, must arise voluntarily from the heart to be what they purport to be.

Compassion, made compulsory, ceases to be compassionate. Morality, much less moral.

Politeness, made mandatory, is no longer considerate. Generosity, required, not so.

———

Coercion drains virtue dry of free will, thus rendering virtue sadly no longer virtuous.

———

Behind every life lies thousands of alternative-lives-I-could-have-lived.

———

As with Gravity, government force is a constant in life—an inescapable weight.

———

Strength of governmental gravity is a function of mass and distance from voters.

———

A child is like a message in a bottle set afloat on the vast uncharted sea of the future.

———

The joys of self-fulfillment are denied those insulated from the burden of self-reliance.

———

Without the freedom to strive and fail, joy of self-realization is denied. Set folks free.

Every change becomes a new status quo despised by the inevitable new generation.

The seemingly formidable "Status Quo" is a sand castle waiting for a new incoming tide.

If you yearn for every heart to be filled with love, let that process begin within your own.

Cultivate an indomitable Will to Happiness. Rise above circumstance for peace within.

There is not always a good answer but there is always a best. Try to find and embrace it.

If you would will it to be so for the good of all, accept it as so within your own heart.

Virtues have become conventions because human experience has taught us how to live.

Virtue is good because it is good for us and because it is good, it ultimately prevails.

The lesson life teaches is to consciously relish whatever happiness one has seen.

Boredom & curiosity cannot co-inhabit the same mind at the same time. Be curious.

Cosmic Justice: Bad choices have bad consequences for the faulty chooser.

Cosmic Injustice: bad consequences too often punish those innocent as well.

To do what one ought is virtuous, but to want what one ought is moral (& harder).

Excess is the hallmark of youth; moderation, a matter of maturity...and far too rare then.

Every plan is a prison of sorts; every sure promise, a shackle. Limits are unavoidable.

Expect little empathy from the adult result of an unloved child. Unconcern is default.

The values instilled in children are the best measure of the character of their parents.

―※―

The focus of morality—the ultimate Should—is, and ever should be, The Greater Good.

―※―

Values » Thoughts » Words » Acts » Habits » Character » Destiny. All linked.

―※―

Reason reckons that my happiness is interdependent with happiness of others.

―※―

Virtue works for The Greater Good. Because we all know that, we deem virtue virtuous.

―※―

In this rational universe, we can assume there is utility for The Greater Good in All.

―※―

Where there is an Effect there is a Cause. Where there is a Creation there is a Creator.

―※―

Why does the canary sing? Because it can. Talent, insistent force, has a will of its own.

Nothing is ever as simple as it seems. Self-evident, that sentence proves its own point.

Interest, the gateway to Knowledge, feeds on Context. That is, prior Knowledge.

What we Know determines what we desire to Know. Knowledge is oxygen for Interest.

In almost any human endeavor, Intensity empowers challengers of superior ability.

Genius seldom thrives in a vacuum. Genius is inspired and magnified by its admirers.

It is better to absorb psychic pain—to eat our own angst—than to burden others.

True wisdom is best revealed through habitual prudence in everyday choices.

With sufficient cages, Equality can be imposed on all the beasts of the forest.

It is out of the conflict of opposing visions that all human progress evolves. No peace.

Beware the Master Sin. It magnifies every other sin and corrupts any virtue: Excess!

By not condemning, we are accepting. By accepting, encouraging. Not judging, is.

Shards of Self are shared with others we love who live on when we are gone to share, too.

Our aging Ethos is ebbing from under my sensitive soul like beach sand under my feet.

Despair not. We have come a long way since our brutish dawn and it is yet early morning.

Humankind is now only at the beginning of what we surely are destined to become.

Nothing is quite so essential to a mind at peace as effective management of keys.

Tyranny, history proves, is the default condition of humankind. Be ever vigilant.

If what you have learned does not affect the way you think, what's the value of knowing?

I understand far more than I know yet I also know far more than I understand. Alas!

Pearls are formed, not made—progressively wrapped around irritants 'til they have worth.

Do not all transient things ultimately self-destruct if left to their own dumb destiny?

Do not be frustrated by uncertainty. It is as essential to life as to football and poker.

When Honor is no longer honored, reverence for Truth withers with it. Once lost, dead.

Restraint improves most things. Limiting myself herein to two lines was a test.

"Freedom" suggests absence of restraint. "Liberty" is absence of imposed restraint.

The more intelligent people are, the more responsible they are for their mistakes.

It is far easier to forgive people who are natural-born idiots than intelligent fools.

Be kind to the future you. Sooner you start, the kinder you'll be. In short, think long.

What do you do since retirement? I read, I study, I write. Mostly, I think. Then, I edit.

Expect little success without stress. Our full potentials are never within easy reach.

The closer you get to the essence of things, the closer you approach the elusive Truth.

Ask yourself, what is best for the young? Then, do that if you can to improve our tomorrows.

Tradition is not the Past but its distilled memories of Reality's treasured lessons.

It is not by the harvest you reap that you are judged but by the seeds you plant now.

Whenever cultural norms take for granted any bad practice, they encourage much more of it.

Only Man plans long, capable of seeing beyond the petty particulars of daily existence.

Embrace real progress, but be cautious of all the good that can be destroyed in the process.

Is the totality of Truth merely the sum of random particulars? Or is there far more?

Acting, boiled to essence, is lying for gain —causing others to believe what ain't so.

The more strivers strive, the more lagers lag. Lessons of history are tragically lost on some.

There is no more powerful force for continuity than the immutability of human nature.

Malcontents ever lurk in shadows with their brickbats. All order is oppressive to some.

When Honor is no longer honored, reverence for Truth withers with it … at high cost to all.

To whom is the individual's obligation owed? To all of Humanity: present, past and future.

The antidote to angst is this: strive to be content with all that which you can't control.

To do the right thing is ever honorable. To do so but at great personal cost is truly noble.

When liberties are lost, we'll yearn to return to sweet chaos of a once self-ordered life.

But it will be too late then to do what we should be doing now to preserve liberty left.

Tolerance for dissenting views is inversely proportional to one's power to squelch them.

Each of us chooses his own path guided by the Truth he embraces from his scrambled life.

The question remains unanswered: Is there enough wisdom to sustain a free society?

I don't know. I only think I know. Nobody knows. Every mind is uniquely imperfect.

All Knowledge is fragmentary. All Perception is distorted. Thus, all arguments are selective.

My last fortress against the absurdities of popular culture is my "Amish Defense."

Happiness, I know, is within my purview
IF I just do as I write and don't do as I do!

Whenever I am truly wrong, just let it be. It is far better for Truth to prevail than me.

The eternal war between Is and Ought
always will be fought … and always ought.

When Time ticks again, a whole new Reality
begins, a brand new sum of all that has been.

Who is responsible, the offender or the
offended, for hurt feeling never intended?

You WILL be misjudged. In response, keep on
doing what is right in your own judgement.

We choose our own path through the Truth
we distill from the scrambled clutter of life.

Deep introspection is like spelunking in the
dark caverns of the mind. Treasures await.

All order is imposed at some cost to Liberty.
But without order, alas, Liberty is unbearable.

Wisdom is found among all the classes: the
educated and the uneducated alike. Always.

Wisdom, like a classic masterpiece in marble is achieved one chip of the chisel at a time.

Our wisdom lies deep within us as potential yet unmined, like silver still in the mountain. Dig it?

Cherish each new insight. Insights are the building blocks of wisdom. And wisdom is gold.

AN INSIGHT INTO INSIGHT:

It happens to us all, does it not? The experience of uninvited insights fluttering nervously about in the twilight shadows of our thoughts like ghostly moths, darting softly ever nearer the dim glow of unacknowledged awareness? Suddenly, one brushes briefly against our consciousness and startles us to attention! Mostly, we absently flick away the distraction and return to our trivial pursuits. But what if you snatched one up now and then and pinned it to a board for examination under a microscope? What wonders might we discover about our own thoughts then? That's what I've tried to do in these pages, and found it marvelously enlightening. Try it and see.

FRANK WALTERS

WE ALL GROW WISER WITH AGE. 10 WAYS TO GROW WISER FASTER:

1. **Understand the value of wisdom**

   Wisdom is not about philosophy; it is about wise choices. Wise choices are essential to a good life. So, prize wisdom as you prize a good life.

2. **Don't confuse wisdom with knowledge.**

   Knowledge is the assimilation of fact and truth; wisdom is the best application of knowledge to the challenges of life. Wisdom depends upon knowledge; knowledge is of diminished value without the wisdom to use it wisely. The wise will pursue both.

3. **Know when you don't know**

   Even the most knowledgeable and wise remain ignorant in manifold ways. The wise recognize their own limitations; the foolish act upon ignorance with as much assurance as if they actually know.

4. **Seek out the wisdom you lack from others you trust**

   Learn to recognize wise and trustworthy counselors. Listen to them, and reject the overabundant bad advice of all others, however well-meaning. Study of the works of great minds conditions the ordinary mind to think higher thoughts. Having brushed against great ideas, we become more than we were.

5. **Learn from your own experience**
   Fools repeat mistakes over and over, condemning themselves to little lives. The wise get wiser with each error. Most significant experiences carry a life lesson of value ... if you develop the habit of extracting principles from experience.

6. **Commit to a wise process for choice**
   Here's an elegantly simple process for wise choice: 1. Understand. 2. Think. 3. Do ... And only in that order.

7. **Always take the long view; set goals**
   The long-term, strategic view of life will inevitably pay vast rewards over the more common-place fools approach of ad libbing each choice as it arises, inspired only by the impulse of the moment. Consequences ripple outward from every event. Correctly anticipating consequences leads to wiser choices.

8. **Let faith, principle and rationality rule**

   When faith, principle and rationality rule, you maintain maximum positive control over life's choices. When impulse and emotion rule, life can become like a helpless cork on a turbulent sea ... and unhappiness prevails.

9. **Keep all things in proper perspective and balance. Prioritize.**

   Decide what is truly important and what is not, what comes first and what can wait, then strive to maintain a rational balance among all demands on your life. Make choices neither too soon nor too late.

10. **Almost always moderation is key and excess an enemy of good**

    Though a few things are black and white, most choices of life are a complex mix of good and bad, pros and cons, advantage and disadvantage. In almost every instant, moderation is wiser than either extreme. Weigh carefully, then choose.

IN APPRECIATION OF

My talented grandson, *Joshua Cunningham*, professional creative director who designed this book, cover to cover and managed its production. My appreciation, too, to his talented wife René who provided the scenic sketches.

My closest of all friends, *Dr. Ralph Oliva*, who as professor of communications at Penn State University, knows a thing or two, persisted in urging me to publish this book because he felt passionately that the world needs all the practical wisdom it can absorb.

My treasured friend, *Steven Howard*, noted author of 20 books of his own and son of popular fiction writer, helped me, advised me and encouraged me in the mechanics of getting a book published.

All my dear friends who read my Pearls and, through their praise, gave me confidence that there may be an audience for it.

And, most of all, my dear wife of 67 years, *LaDonna*, who helped and encouraged me all along and would not let me give up when it became increasingly challenging as my eyesight began to fade.

NOTES

MORE NOTES

ABOUT THE AUTHOR

Whence came all these insights? I am 90 now, a great grandfather of 13. That's the source of most of it. I graduated in 1957 from the University of Texas with a bachelor's degree in journalism and advertising. Since, I have worked in advertising and media relations for General Electric and Texas Instruments, the bulk of that with TI. That was a high-intensity, all-absorbing career for 34 years. Upon retirement in 1991, I set about the task of making myself a "more comprehensive man" (a phrase I borrowed).

My decades of retirement have been devoted to family, travel, reading, writing and the study of more than 40 graduate-level home-study courses from The Teaching Company, focused mostly on history, philosophy, religion and ethics. I have written extensively. My writing has included some 16 self-produced books for my own self-discovery, family and friends.

Only now, with this first volume have I summoned the hubris to publish my work for general consumption, and then under the persistent urging of my closest friend who convinced me that many others would find my insights of value. If indeed you do, please consider recommending this book to others and gifting it to those you care about.

FRANK WALTERS